Thug Notes

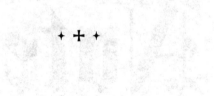

Thug Notes

A STREET-SMART GUIDE TO CLASSIC LITERATURE

SPARKY SWEETS, PhD

VINTAGE BOOKS
A DIVISION OF PENGUIN RANDOM HOUSE LLC
NEW YORK

The Library of Congress Cataloging-in-Publication Data
Sweets, Sparky.
Thug notes : breakin' down the world's best classic lit / by Sparky Sweets, PhD
pages cm
Includes bibliographical references.
1. Best books—Humor.   2. American literature—History and criticism.   3. English literature—History and criticism.   4. Literature and society.   I. Title.
PN6231.B62T48 2015   818'.607—dc23   2015012205

Vintage Books Trade Paperback ISBN: 978-1-101-87304-5
eBook ISBN: 978-1-101-87305-2

Printed in the United States of America
10 9 8 7 6 5 4 3 2 1

✛

**TO MY WELL-READ BALLAS AND
ALL YOU UP-'N'-COMIN' LITERARY HUSTLAS**

✛

All da world's a stage,
And all da men and women . . . playas.

—Shakespeare, *As You Like It*, 2.7.139–140
(remixed by Sparky Sweets, PhD)

✦ ✛ ✦

Contents

✦ ✝ ✦

✌ Introduction ✌

What it do, reader? Name's Sparky Sweets, PhD, and yeah—I like to keep it thug. But you know what? I still keep it **real** in da library. If you ask Webster, a thug ain't nothin' mo' than "a violent criminal." But on da real, da word "thug" got roots in da Sanskrit word *sthagati*, meanin' "he who covers or conceals."

Maybe my bling and G'ed-up swagga **do** hide somethin' 'bout me: my mad love for da classics. Dostoevsky, Dickens, Shakespeare—deez cats are da **real OGs**. So jus' cuz you might see me swangin' down yo' block bangin' chopped-and-screwed music, don't think I couldn't school even da most pretentious literary hustla at his own game.

Lemme lay a story on you. Couple years ago, I rolled up on da university library decked out like a straight balla. I walked up to conversate wit da librarian and girl started buggin' in her seat. Da hell?! Hadn't she seen my ass there erry night porin' over tomes of existentialist theory and comparative analysis? Maybe she couldn't handle da swag?

I put her to da test . . . "Say, where can a brutha find a legit translation of *The Brothers Karamazov*?" "Uh . . . um, excuse me one moment." Da librarian locked her computer **real quick** and headed to da stacks. When she got back, she handed me a book. "Here's *The Brothers Karamazov*," she said.

I grabbed da book and looked it over. "Yo, 'scuse me. This here's Constance Garnett. You got da Pevear and Volokhonsky translation by chance? It's got da elegance, semantic depth, and attention game **sowed up**." Girl gave me a look like, **dayum**. Astonishment. Confusion. Bet she didn't think I even knew deez words. How could I, a black man bustin' a killer sag—a "thug"—possibly know a **damn** thang 'bout nineteenth-century Russian lit?

Dat girl learned real quick not to judge a book by its cover. Sho, I grew up jammin' to NWA, Pac, and Snoop. But I also rock summodat Shostakovich on da reg. I chilled wit' whites, blacks, Asians, Christians, Muslims, Jews—you name it. I grew up on da streets of LA and in da libraries of Compton.

Dat librarian's mess gave me a new mission in life: to wreck da arrogance some literary fools feel like they gotta roll wit'. There's a reason libraries are public. All dem words and stories are for **errybody** to enjoy. To me, literature like a club wit' no line and an open bar 24/7: Anybody can come in and get crunk as they want on dat sweet knowledge joose. Prollem is, a lotta folk don't treat it dat way. Instead, they do da exact opposite: make errything so damn confusin' jus' to sound smart, or to make somebody else sound stupid.

As many a G has asked: Why deez haterz gotta hate? Classic literature is timeless, ageless—and it should be classless. Da whole point of droppin' knowledge is to keep buildin'—for da lit game OGs to help a new crew get on they level, or maybe even higher, not to jus' shit on da peeps who came before you or dat sittin' in front of you.

Deez days, science is pretty damn popular. But even tho da newest gadget or breakthrough study make shit smootha, fasta, and "betta," it cain't fill **all** da holes in our lives. When it come to figgerin' out who we are, who we wanna be, how to treat otha people, and da decisions we gonna make, it's literature dat gonna hook us up. It got da ability to put us in anotha playa's shoes and see da world from different perspectives. It teach us how to empathize and connect wit' othas on a much deeper level, even if they seem different from us.

So why *Thug Notes*? Sometimes people look at me like I lost my damn mind cuz I'm relatin' books to hip-hop culture. So, let's get back to what bein' a thug is: To me, a thug is somebody who buck da system; who stand up and try to make they imprint on da world. A thug live how they **wanna** live, and do what they **wanna** do, even in da face of a world tellin' 'em they gotta act a **certain** way. Most of da novels and authors in this book you holdin' ain't no different. Some of da best works of lit can be thought of as expressions of rebellion or great dissatisfaction wit' da world—existential, political, social, or emotional. And to me, plenty of rappers singin' they heart out 'bout da same thangs: da oppression they face, da troubles wit' they lives, and all da fucked-up shit goin' down in da world around 'em. So how different is dat **really** from any of deez authors? Don't jus' dismiss somethin' cuz it don't look, sound, or feel da way you're used to: There's shit from all ova packed wit' mad meanin'.

So here's my main jam, my illest flow, my Master's Thesis, and my dissertation's argument *pur excellence*:

Learnin' 'bout literature is mo' than jus' memorizin' names, dates, faces, and book summaries—it can broaden our minds and open our hearts by remindin' us not to judge a book by its cover—and ain't nothin' mo' important.

✦ ✝ ✦

𝔚hat 𝔜ou 𝔊onna 𝔉ind in 𝔗his 𝔓iece

Get yo' ass ready for some legit, accurate-as-hell breakdowns of summa literature's dankest works. You ain't only gonna get learned on da characters and what happened in da story, but also on some of da illest themes, symbols, and bits of philosophizin' goin' on between da lines. Afta peepin this book, you'll be straight **turnt up** on literary knowledge.

So enjoy, my well-read ballas.

✦ ✚ ✦

✦ ✛ ✦

Romeo and Juliet

✦ ✦ ✦

⤳ So What's the Deal? ⤳

Check it—this play was written by William Shakespeare, who got street cred for bein' da most turnt-up playa to ever write in da English language and pennin' somma da dopest works eva. This bad bard even **created** 1,700 new words like it ain't no thang. Afta hundreds of years, schola's still got a big ol' hard-on for him. In fact, da only stunna who got more books written 'bout him is Jesus. Dayum. This cat is high balla numba one.

If ever a love story went platinum, it would be *Romeo and Juliet*. Go to yo' corner and ask any hood to name a famous love story and I **bet** they say *Romeo and Juliet*. This play is so off da hook dat people still drop Romeo's name when talkin' 'bout booty-chasin' hustlas. *RJ* also packed wit' somma da most bitchin' themes dat literature got to offer: love, fate, choice, free will . . . I could go on, playa. Of all Shakespeare's jams, *Romeo and Juliet* got more adaptations than Yeezy got rhymes: movies, plays, TV, ballets, paintings, operas . . . you name it, playa. And if you don't know, now you know.

❧ Homies ❧

ROMEO

Da only son of Ol' Montague. This fool only got
one thang on his mind: lovin' da ladies. At da beginnin', he fiendin' to get nasty wit' some choice
hunny named Rosaline. But da second Romeo
meets Juliet, he wanna put a ring on it. Naw mean?
He always in a hurry and actin' without thinkin'.

JULIET

Da Capulets' only child. Apparently, Ol' Capulet and
his boo had otha lil playas, but they all up 'n' died.
At jus' thirteen, Juliet's family already tryn'a get
her hitched to a brutha of they choosin'. Even tho
Juliet usually do what she told, Romeo swipes her
heart, causin' all sorts of mess.

MONTAGUE AND LADY MONTAGUE

Da top dawgs of da Montague House, and da parents of Romeo. Ain't
nothin' they hate mo' than dem Capulets. Mama and Papa Montague
don't do shit in this play, 'cept in da beginnin', when Pops wanna
wreck some scrappy Capulet ass, and at da end, when both crews
flippin' shit 'bout Romeo and Juliet dyin'.

CAPULET AND LADY CAPULET

Juliet's daddy and mama, who be all up in they daughta's bidness.
Ol' Capulet always ridin' Juliet's nuts 'bout gittin' married to Paris.
He even tell her to get da fuck out if she don't do what he say.

BENVOLIO

One of Romeo's main Montague boys. Whenever shit get real in da streets, Benvolio's da one tryn'a keep da peace. A cool-headed homie, Benvolio always serious while Romeo and Mercutio actin' a fool.

MERCUTIO

Romeo's homio who spit some ill verses 'bout love and sex when he tryn'a get Romeo's mind off Rosaline. He ain't 'fraid to talk shit to any hood who cross him or his boys. In fact, he step up when Tybalt talkin' smack to Romeo. Fool ends up gettin' served by Tybalt 'bout halfway through da play.

TYBALT

Juliet's cous'. Fool always tryn'a boot up and throw down for no good reason. Afta killin' Mercutio over some stupid shit, he gets plugged by Romeo. **Street justice!**

PRINCE ESCALUS

Da Big Balla callin' da shots in Verona. He always tweakin' cuz dem punk Montagues and Capulets won't dial back da drama. He ain't pickin' sides cuz he got family in both crews: Mercutio and Paris are his real bloods. Afta Romeo mercs Tybalt, da prince get ice cold and banishes lovaboy.

COUNTY PARIS

Wit' his phat bankroll, slick looks, and good rep, da Capulets see this noble playa as a choice hubby for Juliet. Too bad he's also a candy-ass bitch who get his shit wrecked by Romeo at da end.

FRIAR LAURENCE

A holy man in da Order of Saint Francis. He think he doin' righteous deeds by marryin' Romeo and Juliet, and helpin' Juliet fake her death; but on da real, all he do is bring da pain.

NURSE

Since her own baby girl long dead, da nurse lookin' out for Juliet like she her own. At first, she cool wit' Juliet's secret romance. But once Tybalt get shanked, she get scurred and start tellin' Juliet she should hit up Paris and fo'get 'bout Romeo.

∽ What Went Down? ∽

Up in da swanky part of Verona, two hood-rich families called da Montagues and da Capulets been beefin' since back in da day. Ain't nobody know why, but both of dem gangs always walkin' 'round town, strapped up, jus' waitin' for a reason to start shit.

When two scrub-level Capulets named Samson and Gregory catch a whiff of some punk-ass Montagues rollin' by, Sammy gets all crunk and lays a big fuck-you on all dem Capulets by bitin' his thumb. Sheeeiit.

All this shit talkin' and thumb bitin' lead to a rumble **in da streets**. But a high-rankin' Montague named Benvolio ain't havin' none of dat, and steps up to stop da brawl. When Tybalt, da baddest and craziest thug of all da Capulets, see da shit goin' down, he gits all up in Benvolio's grill.

Errybody in da hood gettin' all riled up at da scene, and even da

Big Daddies of each family show up and start mad doggin' each otha. Jus' when this scrap 'bout to **blow up**, Prince Escalus drop in and start layin' down da law.

Da Fresh Prince had it wit' deez punks warrin' on his turf. He say if they don't quit this shit, he gonna start bustin' caps. Real talk.

Chill errybody!

Then Lady Montague and Benvolio start conversatin' 'bout her son, Romeo, who been mopin' 'round like a whiny bitch. Benvolio try to cheer him up, but Romeo too busy cryin' 'bout some dip named Rosaline dat he been tryn'a holla at. Benvolio wanna get Romeo's mind on otha ladies, but Romeo's dick only pointin' in one direction.

Then some dumbass servant named Peter roll in tryn'a invite peeps to da Capulet's bangin' party. Thang is, this ign'ant bitch don't know who to invite cuz he cain't even read! So he hit up da first brutha he see to help him get his read on. Turn out, it's dat thug Romeo! And Romeo all geeked up dat Rosaline might be there, so he gonna crash da party wit' his boys Benvolio and Mercutio.

Back at da Capulet crib, Lady Capulet yappin' wit' her baby girl, Juliet. Lady C wanna convince Juliet to marry some stuffy uptown playa named Paris, but Juliet ain't sure she's ready to get tied down yet.

At da party, Tybalt realize dat Romeo and his Montague posse dun crashed his crib, and he 'bout to strap up. But Big Daddy Capulet all like, "Chill, baby. Romeo ain't causin' no drama." Tybalt back down, but put Romeo's name at da top of his shit list.

Errybody else tryn'a get they drank on at da party, but Romeo won't shut da fuck up 'bout Rosaline. Romeo's boys jus' want him to forget this trick, and da best way to do dat is by gettin' laid.

When Romeo peep a glance at da most tappable ass of Juliet across da ballroom, he immediately all like, "Rosaline who?"

Romeo lay da mack down **hard**. In no time at all, Romeo and Juliet are suckin' face. Dat's a playa right there, son. One makeout lata, they batshit crazy in love.

So Romeo roll up to Juliet's balcony, where he starts spittin' his A-game. But no matter how much she holla back, they know dat a

Montague marryin' a Capulet ain't gonna fly in this here world. But they like, "Fuck dat—we gettin' married anyway."

Afta a long night of love talk, Romeo hit up holy man Friar Laurence so he can marry Juliet in secret. Even tho Fry-daddy know he dealin' in some crazy-ass shit marryin' two rich teens whose daddies wanna kill each otha, he thinkin' it might make da families calm da fuck down.

Unfortunately, Tybalt ain't forgot 'bout Romeo showin' his face at da Capulet party, so he send a letter callin' Romeo out. Romeo ain't trippin', so he shake off dat heat and go on wit' his day.

Lata, Benvolio and Mercutio jus' chillin' when Tybalt gets all up in Mercutio's grill. Mercutio start fightin' Tybalt, and Romeo bust in sayin', "Break it up, y'all." But fool only trips up Mercutio, and brutha gets merced by Tybalt. Afta seein' his boy die in his arms, Romeo puts all dat angsty shit aside and straight **ices** Tybalt like a cold-blooded gangsta. Dayum!

But da prince of Verona wadn't playin' when he said no mo' gang violence in his hood. So he banishes Romeo from Verona and say if he even think 'bout comin' back, he gonna get his ass handed to him.

Before Romeo splits, he cries to Friar Laurence, who tell him to man da fuck up. Then Romeo go over to Juliet's spot to get a crack at dat ass before he gotta get da hell outta dodge.

While Romeo and Juliet finishin' up they freak nasty, Lady Capulet and Paris schemin' on how to get Juliet hitched. Afta Romeo peaces out, Big Papa Capulet slides over to Juliet's room and tells her what's up: she gonna marry Paris on Thursday.

Juliet book it to Friar Laurence's so she can get away from Paris and back to Romeo. Luckily, da friar's a man wit' a master plan—Juliet's gotta fake her own death. He gives her some joose dat knock her ass out so cold dat homies think she dead. Afta Juliet's fam put her in da crypt, Romeo can go scoop her up. Friar L send his bro Friar John wit' a message to Romeo, lettin' him know what's 'bout to go down.

Prollem is, Friar John get held up and never makes it to Romeo. So when Romeo's boy Balthasar tell him dat Juliet dead, Romeo think it's **for real**. He get so towe up dat he buy some poison from a broke-ass apothecary and go to Juliet's grave, where he gonna kill himself next to his woman. But when he get there, he peep Paris all sad up on her tomb. Paris blame Romeo for Juliet's death. They bang out and Romeo puts a toe tag on dat scrub.

Afta Romeo peep his hunnyboo Juliet layin' stiff, he throw back summodat poison and give Juliet one last kiss before he dies. When Juliet wake up to see Romeo's dead body, she lose her shit. Juliet even try to get a lil taste of dat poison off his lips. Since dat ain't cuttin' it, she takes Romeo's knife and stabs herself to death.

Only afta all this crazy-ass shit do da Capulets and Montagues decide to stop beefin' and put their differences aside.

✌ Themes 'n' Shit ✌

LOVE: *It's da Shit*

Lots of characters in this play goin' off 'bout romantic love, and ain't none of dem ever sayin' da same damn thang.

> MERCUTIO: Why, is not this better now than groaning for love? Now art thou sociable, now art thou Romeo, now art thou what thou art by art as well as by nature.
>
> (2.3.76–78)

Sometimes, love is da dankest shit in da world; da phattest joint you ever blazed. Romeo get so high off of Juliet's love dat he becomes a new person and start jivin' all different-like, layin' down da illest rhymes of his life.

Once you get a lil taste of dat love, you'll be jonesin' for it hard-core. And erry second you can't get yo' love fix goes by in slo-mo (2.1.156–159).

LOVE: *It Ain't All Gravy*

Some cats see da good, while also knowin' dat it can fuckin' suck.

ROMEO: Love is a smoke made with the fume of sighs,
Being purged, a fire sparkling in lovers' eyes,
Being vexed, a sea nourished with lovers' tears.
What is it else? A madness most discreet,
A choking gall and a preserving sweet.

(1.1.183–187)

In Act 1, Romeo all towe up since Rosaline shut his ass down. When you rollin' on love, ain't nothin' sweeter. But if shit go whack and you have a bad trip, love might not seem worth da pain. It jus' gonna leave you cryin' and cray-cray.

LOVE: *What You Want Ain't Always What You Git*

When most ballas think of *Romeo and Juliet*, they always talkin' up dat freaky-deaky romantic love. But on da real, love between bros and kin also goin' hard up in this mutha. Jus' like errything in the Bard's jacked-up world, ain't nothin' turn out da way homies intend.

Papa Capulet only lookin' out for Juliet when he say she **gotta** marry Paris. If she don't, he gonna kick her ass straight to da curb and cut her off. Cuz of dat, all he do is make this girl desperate for a way out. And as we know, her way out ain't so hot.

You gonna marry Paris or else...

But an you will not wed, I'll pardon you!
Graze where you will, you shall not house with me.

. . .

An you be not, hang, beg, starve, die in the streets,
For, by my soul, I'll ne'er acknowledge thee,
Nor what is mine shall never do thee good.

(3.5.187–195)

As a man of da cloth, Friar Laurence got mad love for all his bruthas and sistas. And helpin' out Romeo and Juliet was his way of tryn'a fix up da broke-ass feud between da Capulets an' da Montagues (2.2.90–92).

Da friar thought he had a primo plan to bring Romeo and Juliet togetha and stop da gangs warrin' wit' each otha. Fool get exactly what he was afta, jus' not da way he was thinkin'. Ain't no way

Romeo woulda' sipped dat deadly sizzurp and killed himself without thinkin' Juliet was dead. And remember—fakin' Juliet's death was part of da friar's master plan. So in one way, he dun really fucked up. But at da same time, afta da friar's plan blow up and Romeo and Juliet layin' in chalk, da Montagues and Capulets ain't bustin' each otha' nuts no mo'. Mad *irony*, ya heard?

✦ SPARKY'S CLASSROOM ✦

"Irony" can mean a few different thangs, and it would be remiss of yo' bitch ass to not give all of dem a lil attention:

a. You sayin' one thang, but really meanin' da opposite.
b. An idea or situation is da opposite of what you expectin'.
c. A character's words or actions ain't fully understood by dat homie—but da audience know exactly what up.

FATE VS. CHOICE: WHO'S RIDIN' DA BEEF?

It take less than four days for shit to go sideways in this here play. Whenever anythin' this nasty happens in so little time, most errybody got da same question: *Why?*

Some scholarly hoods point to line 6 of da Prologue ("A pair of star-crossed lovers take their life") and think it mean dat fate givin' it to Romeo and Juliet raw.

And if you ain't convinced dat fate doin' em straight dirty, jus' peep da redonkulous coincidences dat lead up to they death:

- Big Daddy Capulet's dumb-shit servant jus' so happens to ask **Romeo** to help him read da guest list, makin' Romeo wanna hit up da party to chop game at Rosaline. (1.2)
- Da dame Romeo got eyes for turn out to be da **daughter** of his biggest hater. (1.5)
- Da Fresh Prince decide—at jus' this time—to put his foot down against brawlin' dat's been goin' down on da reg **for years**. (1.1)
- Romeo kills Tybalt **right afta** da prince say "no mo' fightin', bitches," and kick Romeo's ass outta Verona. (3.1)
- Friar John fucks up sendin' Romeo da letter explainin' Juliet's fake death. **How's a brutha gonna fuck up sendin' a letter?** (5.2)
- Juliet wake up from her dirt-nap **right afta** Romeo sips dat poison. (5.3)

Even tho homies might not trip 'bout jus' **one** of deez chances goin' down, even da most skeptical brutha gotta admit dat's a lot of crazy shit for four days! Coincidence? Naw, blood. Looks like fate to this thug.

But maybe fate ain't da only thang to blame. Maybe part of da problem is dat Romeo and Juliet actin' exactly like what they are— fuckin' dumbass kids who make shitty choices.

First, Juliet is practically puttin' out on day one. Even though in 2.1 she say they need to slow shit down, all it take is a little sweet talkin' from mack daddy Romeo to make those panties Niagara Fallin'.

Friar Laurence even tell 'em to slow they damn roll. But deez horny teenagers don't listen. They rush da whole thang and put 'emselves on a fast track to an early grave.

When you ignore so many signs tellin' you to check yo'self, it's no wonder peeps gonna lay da blame on you when shit go south.

BACKWARD SHIT IN A BROKEN WORLD

Ain't nothin' simple and straightforward when it come to Dub Shakes, cuz this fool always puttin' opposites togetha in confusin'-ass ways. Make sense, cuz we live in a confusin'-ass world. Paradox, padna!

When Juliet discover dat Romeo's a Montague, she say, "My only love sprung from my only hate!" (1.5.135)

Da hell?! Juliet jus' said dat da only good and pure person in this world popped outta da only evil and rotten thang she know.

Or when Friar Laurence jivin' all philosophical 'bout good and evil:

Virtue itself turns vice being misapplied,
And vice sometime's by action dignified.

(2.2.21–22)

As he learn lata in da play, even a good deed go bad if you bone da execution. Likewise, even somethin' fucked-up can turn inta somethin' righteous, amirite?

✌ Images 'n' Symbols ✌

SILVER AND GOLD

Ol' Willy Shakes slangin' dat silver and gold all up in this text. And jus' like da ice in yo' grill, silver's where it's at, playboy.

Whenever someone in da play goin' off 'bout silver, they usually talkin' 'bout some trill-ass shit, like in Act 2 when Romeo hear Juliet call his name and say:

Lady, by yonder blessèd moon I vow,
That tips with silver all these fruit-tree tops—
. . .
How silver-sweet sound lovers' tongues by night,
Like softest music to attending ears!

(2.1.149–150; 210–211)

But whenever some playa mentions gold, keep an eye out for some
bunk shit lurkin' behind those words. For example, when Romeo
cough up da cash to buy poison, he say da gold change he tossin' da
apothecary is da real evil.

There is thy gold—worse poison to men's souls,
Doing more murder in this loathsome world,
Than these poor compounds that thou mayst not sell.
I sell thee poison; thou hast sold me none.

(5.1.80–83)

And when Romeo bitchin' 'bout exile, he say it ain't so different
from takin' a golden axe to da dome.

Calling death "banishèd"
Thou cutt'st my head off with a golden axe,
And smil'st upon the stroke that murders me.

(3.3.21–23)

Light/Darkness

Let me lay this quote on you, B—

I have no joy of this contract tonight.
It is too rash, too unadvised, too sudden,
Too like the lightning which doth cease to be
Ere one can say it lightens.

(2.1.159–162)

Lightning, light, da stars, da moon, and a whole buncha otha shiny shit surrounded by darkness reppin' da love of Romeo and Juliet throughout da play: cray-cray, intense, fleetin', and surrounded by haterz who wanna break 'em off.

Books

Peep this motif, blood. Images of books poppin' up left and right in Willy Shakes's playground.

When Lady Capulet pimpin' Paris to her baby girl, she talk 'bout 'em shackin' up like slappin' a cover on a book.

This precious book of love, this unbound lover,
To beautify him only lacks a cover.
The fish lives in the sea, and 'tis much pride
For fair without the fair within to hide.
That book in many's eyes doth share the glory
That in gold clasps locks in the golden story.
So shall you share all that he doth possess
By having him, making yourself no less.

(1.3.89–96)

With his fine looks, swole dollas, and solid rep, Paris got it all. And like any good book, he gonna need a tricked-out cover (Juliet) to be on top. Naw mean?? Cuz Lady C sayin' dat once Juliet (da golden clasps) tie da knot wit' this hustla (da golden story), she gonna share his legit street cred.

> JULIET: Was ever book containing such vile matter
> So fairly bound? O, that deceit should dwell
> In such a gorgeous place!
>
> (3.2.83–85)

When Juliet find out dat Romeo put Tybalt in da ground, she cain't believe dat someone so fine could have somethin' so jacked-up on da inside. As our forefathers asked: Did ever a perfect ass produce such stank?

❧ Say What? ❧

Classic

When da chorus breakin' it down for us at da beginnin':

> CHORUS: In fair Verona, where we lay our scene,
> From ancient grudge break to new mutiny,
> Where civil blood makes civil hands unclean.
> From forth the fatal loins of these two foes
> A pair of star-crossed lovers take their life,

Whose misadventured piteous overthrows
Doth with their death bury their parents' strife.

(Prologue 2–8)

REMIX

c: Up in Verona,
two families hatin' on each otha since foreva.
A lil thug from each gang gonna die,
and cuz of dat, those crews gonna stop beefin'.

✦ ✦ ✦

Classic

When Romeo hear dat Rosaline don't wanna get nasty wit nobody:

BENVOLIO: Then she hath sworn that she will still live chaste?
ROMEO: She hath, and in that sparing makes huge waste;
For beauty starved with her severity
Cuts beauty off from all posterity.
She is too fair, too wise, wisely too fair,
To merit bliss by making me despair.
She hath forsworn to love, and in that vow
Do I live dead, that live to tell it now.

(1.1.210–217)

REMIX

B: Rosaline won't put out?
R: Word. Ain't dat some shit?

✦ ✦ ✦

Classic

When Juliet jus' chillin' at home thinkin' 'bout how bad she want Romeo:

> JULIET: O Romeo, Romeo, wherefore art thou, Romeo?
> Deny thy father and refuse thy name,
> Or if thou wilt not, be but sworn my love,
> And I'll no longer be a Capulet.
>
> (2.1.75–78)

REMIX

> J: Why ya gotta be a scrub-ass Montague?
> Drop yo name and I'll drop my panties.

◆ ◆ ◆

Classic

At da end of da play, when da Prince fin' out errybody dead:

> PRINCE: . . . Capulet, Montague,
> See what a scourge is laid upon your hate,
> That heaven finds means to kill your joys with love.
> And I, for winking at your discords, too
> Have lost a brace of kinsmen. All are punishèd.
>
> (5.3.290–294)

REMIX

> PRINCE: You guys are dicks.
> I'm a pussy.
> And we all got fucked.

To Kill a Mockingbird

✦ ✚ ✦

∼ So What's the Deal? ∼

If you eva wonda'd what thuggin' in da 1930s American South was like, look no mo', playboy: Harper Lee's *To Kill a Mockingbird* got rep for some of da realest talk 'bout da racist shit dat went down back then.

It also got some of da most memorable characters in all da literature game—Atticus Finch, for one. Even tho errybody in town hatin' on him since he defendin' a black man, Atticus keep on truckin' and don't let dem ign'ant racists keep him down.

Not only dat, but when this book hit da streets, it climbed da charts faster than Beyoncé. This shit even won a Pulitzer Prize preachin' dem universal themes of tolerance, courage, compassion, and justice—no matta' how much hate come yo' way.

⮜ Homies ⮞

JEAN LOUISE FINCH (SCOUT)

A lil white girl livin' in Alabama. Her pops, Atticus,
been schoolin' her since she was shittin' in diapers,
so Scout way smarta' than all da otha lil thugz she
in class wit'. She also got bigga balls than most
of da boys she know; erry time some lil kid talk
smack to her, she quick to throw down. Haterz always tellin' Scout she gotta dress and act mo' lady-
like, but girl do her own thang. Respect.

JEREMY FINCH (JEM)

Scout's olda brutha by four years. Jem and Scout always gettin' into
some kinda trouble. Like Scout, Jem come to see da world in a whole
new way afta learnin' dat in the racist south, "justice for all" only
apply if yo' skin da right color.

ATTICUS FINCH

Scout and Jem's daddy, and all-around legit-ass lawyer. While errybody else in town hatin' on black folk for no good reason, Atticus
step up and defend a brutha when nobody else will. Atticus believe in true street justice—none of this southern white-supremacy
bullshit. This fool got mad brains and a heart of gold to match.

ARTHUR "BOO" RADLEY

Errybody in town spreadin' rumors 'bout this fool on da reg, cuz he
a holed-up shut-in dat ain't nobody seen in years. But in a town full

of crackas who convict a black man jus' cuz of da color of his skin, maybe stayin' inside ain't such a bad idea.

TOM ROBINSON

Da po' black man who get accused of a crime, when on da real, he didn't even do nothin'. Da charge? Tryn'a dip his pen in some white ink. Naw mean?!

BOB EWELL

A weak-ass honkie who errybody in da hood cain't stand since he always sippin' on dat crunk joosc all day erry day. Fool catch his daughter tryn'a get sweet on Tom Rob, gives her five across the face, and then make up some bullshit 'bout how T-Robinson try to rape her. Fool is a first-class bitch.

CHARLES BAKER HARRIS (DILL)

A lil thug in Jem and Scout's posse. He got a crazy-ass imagination, and always tellin' stories 'bout Boo Radley.

MAYELLA EWELL

Bob Ewell's lonely-as-fuck daughter who always hollerin' at Tom Robinson cuz she want some of dat sweet chocolate. When Mayella try to sit on T-Rob's face, he keep it real and tell her to step. But Mayella go Queen Bitch on his ass and try to throw Tom's ass in da clink by sayin' he raped her.

CALPURNIA

Calpurnia work for da Finch family and know two thangs: how to cook and how to keep it real. When Scout step outta line, Calpurnia always put her in check real fast. She also help dem kids see dat black folk and white folk ain't so different.

⟶ What Went Down? ⟵

Up in da boonies of Alabama (in some made-up trap call Maycomb), a lil girl named Scout and her older brutha, Jem, kickin' it in they country-style digs wit' they black cook, Calpurnia, and they daddy, Atticus. Atticus on da grind erryday lawyerin' like a G, and always preachin' 'bout gettin' da underdog's back. When summer come 'round, a lil bruh by da name of Dill move in on da block and start chillin' wit' Scout and Jem 24/7.

Since there ain't shit to do in Alabama, one day Scout and her crew decide they gonna start messin' wit' a shut-in named Boo Radley, who ain't nobody seen for years. Scout give us da 411 on Boo. Apparently, he got into a little trouble wit' da law: homie shanked his daddy wit' some scissors, and now his family put his ass on lockdown in their stuff-ass digs. House arrest for shankin' somebody with scissors? Dat wouldn't be how it go down if Boo was black!

So Scout and her homies head ova there to try to harrass a brutha, but they too scurred to actually do nothin'.

Summer end, and Scout gotta start hittin' up da books at school. 'Cept when she get there, her teacher, Ms. Caroline, hatin' on her cuz she way smarter than all da otha lil dumb shits in her class. When it time for da kids to get they grub on, one lil hood name Walter Cunningham ain't got nothin' to eat. Scout try to explain to her teach dat Walter's so cashed out dat da Cunninghams cain't give him no munchies. But Ms. Caroline tired of Scout's lip and jus' keep treatin' her like shit.

Scout get crunk on Walter's ass for gettin' her in trouble, but Jem tell her to back down; then he invite Walter ova to eat at they spot. When Walter get to they crib and start grubbin', he dumps like a whole bottle of Aunt Jemima on his food. Scout call him out for eatin' like a po'-ass scrub, and Calpurnia smack her up real good. Then Calpurnia tell Scout dat she **sho as hell** ain't betta than nobody if all she gonna do is hate. Preach!

One afta'noon, Scout roll by da Radley crib and notice someone dun left gum and a couple ol' pennies in a tree out front. Dat some weird shit right there. Scout boosts dat shit, and Jem and Dill start hustlin' to try 'n' sneak a peek at Boo. Jem and his posse don't lurk 'round da Radley digs too much longa, tho—somebody come outta da house wit' a shotgun and start bustin' caps! Errybody get the hell outta there **real fast**.

A lil while lata, Scout find some mo' weird shit layin' in da front of da Radley spot. This time, somebody left out some little creepy soap figurines of Jem and Scout, a pocket watch, and a medal.

Lata, some shit goin' down in da hood when they neighbor Miss Maudie's house in a **blaze** and erryone in town gatherin' to see it happen. Scout gettin' a lil cold outside, but some mystery playa sneak up behind her and hook a sista up by puttin' a blanket 'round her. Atticus all like: "Say, kids. You betta thank Boo Radley for givin' you dat blanket." Jem and Scout like: **Dafuq?**

Back at school, Scout 'bout to get in a tussle with some lil fool afta he open his big mouth and say Scout's daddy, Atticus, like "defendin' niggaz." Apparently, Atticus dun stepped up to da plate defendin' a righteous thug named Tom Robinson, who been wrongly accused of rapin' local white girl Mayella Ewell.

As Tom Robinson's trial nearin', Scout peeps some hoods maddoggin' Atticus to try and scare him away from defendin' Tom. But Atticus ain't no bitch. He shake dem haterz off.

ATTICUS DON'T GIVE A FUCK.

Up at da trial, Scout, Jem, and Dill try to fine some seats, but they ain't no room wit' da whitefolk, so they gotta sit in da "colored section." Accordin' to crooked-honkie-of-the-year Bob Ewell, he heard his daughta screamin', ran his ass ova to a window, and peeped Tom Robinson gettin' fresh wit' her before smackin' her up.

Atticus killin' it in da courtroom tho. He go up to Bobby E and be all like, "If that's really how it went down, then why didn't you call a doctor? Huh? Oh, and looks like yo' daughter got bruises on the right side of her face. How dat even **possible** when Tom Robinson's left hand all jacked-up? Say, ain't **you** left-handed?"

When Bob's daughter, Mayella, step up to da plate, Atticus lay down the gauntlet and be all like, "Look, bitch, none of the local boys even heard you scream. Why don't you stop frontin' and tell errybody da truth: There wadn't no rape and yo' **own daddy** beat you." Gettin' called out like dat makes Mayella **bust** into tears and scream, "Y'all jury best not bitch out. Throw dat sucka in da slammer!"

Then Tom Rob take the mic and say, "Look, bruh, sometime dat girl Mayella holla at a brutha and ask me to help her 'round da house. But when I got there, there wadn't nothin' to do. She didn't want me to work on da house, she wanted me to work on **her**." Oh shit, looks like Mayella wanted some some of dat dark chocolate and **she** been da one puttin' da moves on Tom. "Then dat honkie Bobby Ewell saw his daughter tryn'a get freak-nasty wit' me and said **'Bitch, Imma kill you,'** so I got my black ass outta there."

All da otha witnesses Atticus bringin' in say dat Tom always been a solid guy and there ain't no reason to think he eva lay a hand on **any** biddy—white or not. Even tho Atticus dun towe shit **up** in dat courtroom, Tom gets convicted anyway. Why? Cuz he black. There still hope, tho. Atticus thinkin' there be a chance they can win at an appeal.

Yep, things ain't so bad here.

Next day, Jem totally lose his shit. He used to think dat American courtrooms were righteous places where errybody get da same chance. But afta seein' dat trial, he realize jus' how poisonous racism is.

Now word on da street is dat boy Ewell got **major** beef wit' Atticus for makin' him look like a fool up in court. Erryone buggin' thinkin' dat Bob might do somethin', 'cept Atticus, who think Bob jus' flexin'. Wit' all this beefin' goin' down, Jem realize maybe dat why Boo Radley don't leave da crib. Who would want to?

Lata, Scout kickin' back at her auntie's place when word come dat T-Robinson tried to escape from da clink and got his ass capped seventeen times! Excessive force!

Dat Halloween, Jem and Scout head over to a school pageant. On da way home, Jem and Scout get **jumped** by Bob Ewell, who been sippin' a lil too much drank. Bob roughs Jem up **good** and straight breaks his arm, but then someone else come outta nowhere, throw Bob Ewell to da ground, and **kill** his bitch-ass. Then this mystery playa carry Jem back to da crib where they call da doc. Scout look at this cat and realize, "Oh shit. **Boo Radley** jus' saved my ass!"

Sick of all Bob Ewell's bullshit, Atticus and da local po-po jus' say, "You know what? No need to bring da heat down on anyone cuz of this. Let's jus' say dat Bob fell on his knife. Tom Rob died for no reason—and they ain't no reason to put anotha' mockin'bird six feet deep."

∽ Themes 'n' Shit ∽

MERCIFUL DEALIN'S

Back in da day, Atticus was da best shot in town. I mean this brutha was **pro** wit' a gat. But instead of usin' his mad skillz to be da boss 'round town, he decide to keep 'em on da DL.

When da sheriff ask Atticus to help him cap a sick dog, Jem and Scout get all geeked when they hear they daddy's mean wit' a

Glock. Then da Finch's neighbor Miss Maudie tell 'em what up wit' they pops:

> He's civilized in his heart. . . . He put his gun down when he realized that God have given him an unfair advantage over most living things. (98)

Dat's why Atticus always tellin' Scout dat she best watch dat pride and anger. Jus' cuz she can whoop somebody's ass don't mean she should.

So even tho Atticus fightin' tooth and nail to keep ol' T-Rob outta da big house, he still feel like he doin' Mayella raw by callin' her out in front of errybody to get to da truth (188).

EMPATHIZIN' AND SYMPATHIZIN'

They ain't nothin' easier than hatin' on somebody jus' cuz they different. And dat's what Scout seein' in all da local Alabama hoods. As Atticus tell her:

> If you can learn a simple trick, Scout, you'll get along a lot better with all kinds of folks. You never really understand a person until you consider things from his point of view . . . until you climb into his skin and walk around in it. (30)

If you try to look at da world from somebody else's eyes, you gon recognize they ain't so different—and dat exactly what Scout realize through all dat mess wit' Tom Rob and Boo Rad.

When Scout get her **soul** on wit' Calpurnia up in da black church, she finally able to look at life through da eyes of dem Alabama black folk. Also, at da end, when Scout walk wit' Boo Radley up to his porch and look out like he do, she able to betta understand his situation. She realize dat "Atticus was right":

> One time he said you never really know a man until you stand in his shoes and walk around in them. Just standing on the Radley porch was enough. (279)

COURAGE

This a different kind of courage than people usually goin' off 'bout. Scout and Jem think Daddy high-ballin' cuz he got a piece in his hand, but Atticus tell dem kids dat courage ain't jus' 'bout packin' heat. Real courage is when "you're licked before you begin . . . and you see it through no matter what" (112).

Atticus rockin' dat same tho'ed-up courage when he defendin' Tom Robinson:

> Sometimes we have to make the best of things, and the way we conduct ourselves when the chips are down. . . . Scout, I couldn't go to church and worship God if I didn't try to help that man. (104)

Ain't nothin' easier than hatin' on a homie when erryone in yo' town doin' it. But a true playa strapped with a big dick of courage don't jus' follow da pack; he nuts up, shakes off dem haterz, and do what he know is right.

✌ Images 'n' Symbols ✌

JEM'S LEFT ELBOW

Now you mighta fo'gotten dat at da beginnin', Scout tell us dat her older bruh, Jem, got his arm fucked up. And even tho she don't jive 'bout it much afta dem first couple pages, it's one of da most important symbols up in here (3).

First off, he ain't the only bruh with a busted-up left arm in this story. Dat playa Tom Robinson also got his left arm jacked up in a cotton gin when he was a lil boy. Even though Jem cain't walk a mile in Tom's shoes, he can at least put one of 'em on.

Dat broken arm also reppin' the broken American justice system. Cuz truth is, in this whack-ass time, homies who lookin' for justice end up gettin' crippled by da system. Tom was definitely innocent, but fool still gotta ride the beef for it.

Jus' like Jem gotta roll wit' dat jacked-up arm for da rest of his days, dat injustice is something America's gonna have to tussle wit' for a long-ass time to come. Like Atticus say:

> They've done it before and they did it tonight and they'll do it again and when they do it—seems that only children weep. (213)

GHOSTIN'

Peeps always goin' off 'bout Boo Radley like he more than jus' some crazy shut-in . . . like he a ghost or somethin'. First off, er-ryone on da streets know him as **Boo** Radley, even tho his mama call him Arthur. Matta fact, there be all sorta images comparin' him to a ghost. Peep this:

- ◆ Boo called a **"malevolent phantom."** (9)
- ◆ "Nobody knew what form of intimidation Mr. Radley employed to keep Boo out of sight . . . [but] there were other ways of making people into ghosts." (11)
- ◆ Plus da book Atticus readin' to Scout at the end called *The Gray Ghost* (281).

What really goin' on here is dat Atticus hammerin' home da fact dat you can't be lookin' **through** people, padna. You gotz to look **at** and **inside** 'em.

MOCKINGBIRD

What you know 'bout this book's title? Miss Maudie lay down some real talk 'bout mockingbirds, sayin':

Mockingbirds don't do one thing but make music for us to enjoy. They don't eat up people's gardens, don't nest in corn-cribs, they don't do one thing but sing their hearts out for us. That's why it's a sin to kill a mockingbird. (90)

And when Atticus ask Scout if she understan' why they gotta lie 'bout how Ewell died, Scout say, "Sho nuff," and dat it would be jus' like poppin' a cap in a mockingbird's rhyme-bustin' ass (276).

We live in a world where real gangsta shit go down all da time. Da biggest tragedy is when somethin' like a mockingbird get caught in da crossfire, cuz dem lil homies ain't never do anythin' bad to no one.

Any kinda justice dat takin' down mockingbirds ain't no justice at all.

～ Shout-Outs! ～

Givin' props to otha works dat preachin' da same truths as *To Kill a Mockingbird*.

Classic

I do not ask the wounded person how he feels, I myself become the wounded person.

—Walt Whitman, "Song of Myself"

REMIX

Words only gonna tell you so much 'bout how a brutha or sista feel. You gotta step into they shoes, playboy.

✦ ✦ ✦

Classics

Whenever you are about to find fault with someone, ask your-self the following question: What fault of mine most nearly resembles the one I am about to criticize?

—Marcus Aurelius, *Meditations*

Cowards die many times before their deaths,
The valiant never taste of death but once.
Of all the wonders that I yet have heard
It seems to me most strange that men should fear,
Seeing that death, a necessary end,
Will come when it will come.

—William Shakespeare, *Julius Caesar* 2.2.32–37

REMIX

Da Finch kids get to learn 'bout legit courage from mo' than one homie in this novel. Atticus make damn sure dat they know dat what's **right** is a helluva lot mo' important than lookin' out for numba one.

Pride
and
Prejudice

✦ ✛ ✦

∽ So What's the Deal? ∽

There ain't many authors dat been dead for over a hundred years who got da hard-core fan followin' Jane Austen got. Sheeeiit, not only do she got book clubs all ova da country, but she even got **movies 'bout her book clubs**—and a movie 'bout a Jane Austen **theme park**. People are wild 'bout this girl! And prolly da biggest reason is *Pride and Prejudice*, her most famous work.

> Now I ain't sayin' she a gold digger, but she ain't messin' wit' no broke niggaz.
>
> —Kanye West, "Gold Digger"

Lil didja know dat one of Yeezy's tightest flows perfectly describe this novel: a book 'bout a bunch of ladies tryn'a shack up wit' dudes who got swole pockets. Set in nineteenth-century British high society, we watch a buncha women hustlin' to make sure dat da world don't do 'em dirty and leave 'em out without summodat cheddar.

Now, ain't nobody know if Austen was throwin' shade at a cash-obsessed society where women jus' chasin' grands, or if she actually support it. She slangin' her own special kind of irony dat schola's been geekin' out 'bout for years, addin' multiple layers of meanin' to erry page.

❧ Homies ❧

LIZZY BENNET

Packin' way mo' brains than her four otha sistas, Lizzy don't take shit from nobody and always callin' people out for bein' assholes. When Darcy start givin' her lip at da beginnin', she like, "Fuck dat playa—I don't give a damn how thick his paper be." But as da book go on, Lizzy start thinkin' she mighta jumped da gun judgin' dat fool. It take a while for Lizzy to learn she need to slow her roll and give a brutha a chance.

FITZWILLIAM DARCY

Da hunnies all up on this rich playboy and he know it. Darcy don't want nothin' to do wit' hoodrats who ain't got da rep and stacks he got. But truth is, he ain't such a hard-ass. He know there are mo' important thangs than jus' class and cash, even tho he don't show dat to errybody. Dude get dissed by Lizzy when he propose, but he keep it gangsta and keep showin' her dat he da real deal. At da end of the novel, he finally get a crack at dat ass.

CHARLES BINGLEY

As anotha rich white boy strapped wit' so much of dat green, he got da pick of da pussy-litter. When he buy a **phat** mansion near da Bennet crib, he got da pick of all dem Bennet girls too. Even tho erryone tellin' him he best marry rich, he decide he gonna do his own thang when he start hollerin' at Lizzy's sista Jane. Dude get cock-blocked by Darcy and his own sista, but eventually nut up and marry Jane.

JANE BENNET

Oldest of da Bennet girls, and also da finest. She fall hard for Bingley and get all towe up when he stop hollerin'. S'all good at da end tho, cuz she and Bingley shake off da haterz and get married.

MRS. BENNET

As mama of da Bennet girls, she only got one thang on her mind—get her daughters to marry somebody who rich as fuck. And she gonna do whateva it take to make dem rich folk see her daughtas, even if it mean makin' a complete ass of herself.

MR. BENNET

Big Daddy of da Bennet household. Fool cain't stand mama Bennet actin' like a damn fool, and he let da whole world know it by dissin' her on the reg. Lizzy his favorite, cuz she got balls even bigger than his.

LYDIA BENNET

Youngest and stoopidest daughter of all da Bennets. She almost fuck up da entire family's street cred when she run off wit' Wickham before they even married. Scandalous!

GEORGE WICKHAM

A soulja boy who throw on dat charm and chop game at Lizzy like he interested. But turn out, all this fool doin' is chasin' paper. Lata, he shit in errybody's cereal when he elope wit' Lydia and hold' her reputation for ransom. Dude lies his ass off, hooks up wit' hoes jus' for they stacks, and end up jus' fine in the end: married and with bling. Not bad, George. Not bad.

MR. COLLINS

Mr. Bennet's cous' who 'bout to inherit da Bennet family fortune jus' cuz he got a dick. First he try to marry Lizzy, but once she shut his ass down, he jus' throw himself at da closest piece of ass he see: Lizzy's friend Charlotte.

THE GARDINERS

Mama Bennet's brutha and sista, who hustled hard for they Benjamins. They always lookin' out for Lizzy and got her back for life. Deez hoods help teach Darcy dat "high-class" ain't determined by no dolla' sign.

❧ What Went Down? ❧

Mr. and Mrs. Bennet sho got a lotta work to do. They got five kids, all girls, and none of 'em got a man. Shiiiiit. Mrs. Bennet's main goal in life is to make sho her girls, Lizzy, Jane, Lydia, Mary, and Catherine (Kitty), shack up wit' men who got a whole lotta dough. So when word come dat some rich cat Charles Bingley jus' bought a **phat** crib in da hood, Mrs. Bennet tell her daughtas they best get ready to buss dat ass, cuz any hood who got mad grands must be lookin' for a wife, amirite?

Lata, all da girls hit up da club, errybody gettin' tipsy, and Bingley and his main homeboy, Fitzwilliam Darcy, puttin' it down like a couple of creased-up gangstas.

Bingley sneak a peek at Lizzy's sista Jane, and he like, **"Dat ass tho!"** He throw some moves her way and they spend da whole night bumpin' and grindin' on da dance flo'. Then Bingley go up to Darcy and be all like, "Yo, man, do a brutha a solid and dance wit' Lizzy. Be my wingman, naw mean?" But Darcy all like, "Dat ugly bitch right there? You my boy, but we ain't **dat cool**." Lizzy hear him talkin' down and be like, "Oh, hell naw. Imma remember dat."

One day, Jane get word dat Bingley's fam wanna see her over at they swag pad. Knowin' it 'bout to rain, Mama Bennet send Jane ova there wit'out no carriage, so dat once it start porin' down, Jane will have to crash at da Bingley crib. Thang is, Jane end up gettin' sick from truckin' it in da cold-as-a-bitch rain. Now Jane so sick in bed dat ain't nobody wanna hit it. When Lizzy hear dat her sista's sick as hell, she hoof it ova to Bingley's and take care of Jane. But Lizzy sho as hell didn't expect to see Darcy's smug-ass mug there, who start eye-fuckin' her errytime they in da room togetha. Da hell?

Afta Lizzy and Jane get back from da Bingley spot, some holy-rollin' clergyman name Mr. Collins swang inta town. See, Mr. Bennet only got daughters, and this weak-ass English society ain't gonna let women inherit they daddy's money. So Mr. B gotta give it to his cousin Mr. Collins, since he da next dude in da bloodline. Mr. Collins got eyes for Jane's fine self and start tryn'a lay dat mack down, but catches word dat she and Bingley got a little somethin' somethin' goin' on. So Mistah C moves on to numba two: Lizzy.

Shit really heat up when anotha brutha roll inta town: some soulja name Wickham. Jus' 'bout erry skirt in da hood all up on dat fool's nuts—even Lizzy for a little while. Lizzy chill wit' Wickham a bit, and learn dat he and Darcy got beef. Shady. Accordin' to Wickham, Darcy's daddy meant to leave him a swole fortune in his will, but Darcy did some shysty shit on da down-low and kept all da money to himself. Lizzy already think Darcy's a chump, so Wickham gotta be spittin' da truth.

Afta anotha Bingley party where Lizzy's fam make theyselves look like some real assholes in front of God, Darcy, and da whole damn world, Collins decide he gonna take it next-level: he ask Lizzy if she wanna marry him. Lizzy like, "Naw, blood. Thanks tho." Mama Bennet get all bent when she hear Lizzy shut down da man who gonna get all da Bennet cash and land. Mr. Bennet jus' like, "Don't listen to yo mama. Do yo thang."

A little lata, Jane get a letter dat Bingley and his crew gettin' outta town and ain't never comin' back. Jane feel like she got **played**. Not only dat, but turn out Collins got tired of chasin' Lizzy and moved on to her friend Charlotte Lucas. Mama Bennet 'bout to shit a brick. Now **two** of her girls ain't got no chance of gettin' hitched.

Thankfully, it ain't all bad for Mama B, cuz her badass bro, Mr. Gardiner, come to town wit' his woman. They decide to take Jane to London to clear her head, since she depressed as shit afta gettin' burned by Bingley. Before da Gardiners go, Mrs. Gardiner get straight-up wit' Lizzy 'bout Wickham: "Girl. I don't care how hot he be. Fool broke as a joke." Don't matter tho, cuz not only do Lizzy realize she ain't really interested in gettin' down wit' Wickham, but we fine out dat fool already afta some new ass. Playa.

Lizzy decide she gonna hit up her girl Charlotte, who now livin' wit' her lame-ass hubby, Mr. Collins. They crew get invited to visit Mr. Collins's boss, Lady Catherine de Bourgh, who actually Darcy's aunt. Lizzy hear dat Darcy been braggin' dat he saved one of his homeboys from marryin' a hoodrat wit' no street cred. Lizzy put two and two togetha, and think dat **Darcy been talkin' shit 'bout Jane and the Bennets.** Lata, Lizzy marinatin' on dat fucked-up news when Darcy bust in and be like, "Lizzy! I love you! Lemme show you why they call me Big Willy D, girl." But Lizzy like, "Fuck you, playboy. You cock-blocked my sista, makin' you numba one on my shit list. Plus, you hustled Wickham outta some dough. Deuces, prick."

So Darcy slip Lizzy a letter sayin': "Yeah, I mighta fucked thangs up wit' Jane and Bingley. My bad. Thang is tho, I did it for my boy, cuz yo' sista didn't show no interest in him. I jus' didn't wanna see my boy get his heart jacked up." Dat letter also set da record straight 'bout his beef wit' Wickham, and it go like this: Wickham **did** get dat cash-money from Darcy's pops, but he

~~MUFF BLOCK, CLAM JAMMER~~

COCK BLOCK

~~BUSH WHACKER, TACO BLOCKO~~
~~TWAT SWAT~~

wanted mo': so he tried to mack on Darcy's **sista**, Georgiana, jus' so he could get his grubby hands on da rest of dem family grands. Now Lizzy feel like Queen Bitch for goin' off on Darcy when she only know half da story.

Lata, da Gardiners ask Lizzy to join 'em on a trip to Pemberley, where Darcy's swole digs be; Lizzy only agree to go since Darcy ain't s'posed to be at home. When Lizzy tourin' da crib, she admit it would be pretty sweet to roll 'round in this kinda' swag erry day; and, she start hearin' all deez stories 'bout how nice Darcy actually is. Da hell? Dat ain't da Darcy **she** know.

Outta nowhere, Darcy show up, but instead of bein' an ass to Lizzy, he act all suave. Dude even bring his sista over so she and Lizzy can chill. Jus' 'bout errybody realize Darcy got a hard-on for Lizzy, and Lizzy really warmin' up to da dude. Good times don't last, tho: Lizzy get a letter sayin' dat her sis Lydia jus' skipped town wit' Wickham, so she gotta book it back home.

Since Wickham ain't put a ring on it yet, da Bennets tweakin' out cuz they whole family's rep 'bout to go down the shitter; and now Lizzy worried dat she got no chance wit' Darcy. Lydia and Wickham eventually get married, but only cuz somebody gave Wickham a buncha dead presidents. Da Bennets thinkin' Uncle Gardiner stepped in and did 'em a solid.

Lydia's V-card

𝕿𝖍𝖚𝖌 𝕷𝖎𝖋𝖊

Turn out, tho, it wadn't Mr. Gardiner dat tracked Wickham down and paid him—it was **Darcy**. Lizzy all kinda confused now.

Lata, Bingley start showin' his face at da Bennet house again and eventually say, "Look, Jane, I've been a dumb ass fool. Marry me!" Jane like, **"For sho, baby."**

Then it Lizzy turn to get a visitor: Lady Catherine. Huh? Word on da street, accordin' to Lady C, is dat Darcy thinkin' 'bout droppin' da question to Lizzy. Lizzy play it cool, but on da inside, she 'bout to flip shit. Lady Catherine get **all** up in Lizzy's grill tellin' her to back off Darcy, but Lizzy jus' tell dat bitch to step. She do what she want.

Afta Lizzy send dat rich bitch home, Darcy drop inta town and lay da mack down on Lizzy again. When he propose, she say yes this time. Look like errything all good for dem girls.

✎ Themes 'n' Shit ✎

PRIDE 'N' PREJUDICE
Pride

To most, it pretty clear dat da title referrin' to Darcy and Lizzy—dat Darcy reppin' pride and Lizzy reppin' prejudice.

At first, it Darcy who sippin' on dat pride joose, cuz he thinkin' he too good for errybody, includin' Lizzy. It take all of three seconds for errybody in da club to realize this fool a first-class asshole:

He was the proudest, most disagreeable man in the world, and everybody hoped that he would never come there again. (50)

Lizzy ain't havin it wit' dat bullshit, and she let him know it too. Girl get **real crunk** on his ass and call him arrogant, conceited, selfish, and da last chump she'd eva get down wit' (214).

But there be two thangs Lizzy and peeps jus' ain't gettin: first—we all got a lil bit of pride. Darcy ain't da only one who actin' a fool like dat. Sheeeiit, even Lizzy got a big ol' head cuz she think she can size up a playa and know what he all 'bout jus' by lookin' at him (226).

Second, pride **don't hafta** be a bad thang:

> It [had] often led [Darcy] to be liberal and generous, to give his money freely, to display hospitality, to assist his tenants, and relieve the poor. (115)

Prejudice

Lizzy da kinda biddy who always judgin' people real quick and stickin' to it. When she conversatin' wit' her sista Jane, we see Lizzy ain't da biggest fan of yo' average hood (53). A lil lata, Lizzy start goin' even harder and straight lay it out for Jane:

> There are few people whom I really love, and still fewer of whom I think well. The more I see of the world, the more am I dissatisfied with it. (164–165)

Her future boy toy Darcy got his own issues with prejudice, and ain't got no problem bein' straight up 'bout it. You piss dat fool off, you show up on his shit list for good (93).

So in da end, da word "pride" don't jus' refer to Darcy, and da word "prejudice" don't jus' refer to Lizzy. Nah, blood, it a lot mo' complicated than dat. Both of dem characters, jus' like errybody, got a lil pride and a lil prejudice.

JUS' CUZ YOU MARRIED DON'T MEAN YOU HAPPY

Jus' cuz da book end wit' Lizzy shackin' up wit da hood-rich Darcy, do that make it a happy ending?

When you look at how da text talk 'bout marriage, it hard to say whether it a good thang. To Lizzy's homegirl Charlotte, bein' happy and married is a coin toss: You barely know each otha before you're hitched, and afta you shack up, you might learn you married a real asshole (60-61).

Then afta decidin' to marry Collins, she say dat all she care 'bout was how his solid rep and cash flow gonna make her life comfortable (154–155).

Even Lizzy's mom and pops sippin' dat same Kool-Aid. Turns out dat all da crazy shit comin' outta Mama's mouth made Lizzy's dad check out a looooong time ago:

> Respect, esteem, and confidence, had vanished for ever; and
> all his views of domestic happiness were overthrown. (250)

CLASS

Dem Bennet girls grindin' hard to find some ends cuz all they daddy's money is goin' to Mr. Collins.

When you thuggin' in a society dominated by class, there ain't nothin' harder than tryn'a get in da pants of somebody on a different social level than you. And dat don't go for jus' da po' ones tryn'a tap dat rich ass. It go da otha way too: even da hood-rich gotta face dat problem. For Darcy, mo' money **actually do mean** mo' problems, cuz dat rich girl Lady Catherine think Darcy gonna be a piece of shit if he marries Lizzy's po' self (359).

But class ain't jus' 'bout how much paper you stackin'. And Darcy's beef wit' Lizzy's family ain't jus' a money thang: It's cuz they always actin' a damn fool—'specially Mama Bennet. Like Darcy write in a letter to Lizzy:

> [T]here were other causes of repugnance. . . . The situation [social class] of your mother's family, though objectionable, was nothing in comparison to that total want of propriety so frequently, so almost uniformly betrayed by herself, by your three younger sisters, and occasionally even by your father. (218)

BEIN' BLIND TO WHAT'S GOOD AND KNOWIN' YO'SELF

Afta Darcy get his ass shut down by Lizzy, he send her a letter tellin' her what's really up. At first, Lizzy don't give a damn 'bout what he has to say, but afta readin' da letter, she recognize dat she been judgin' him all wrong (223, 224).

Even tho Lizzy was actin' all uppity thinkin' she could judge people, she ain't able to judge herself. How you gonna call out someone else's mistakes if you cain't even see yo' own? Naw mean?

> "How despicably have I acted!" she cried. "I, who have prided myself on my own discernment!—I, who have valued myself on

my abilities! who have often disdained the generous candour of my sister, and gratified my vanity, in useless or blameable distrust! . . . Till this moment, I never knew myself." (226–227)

Lizzy ain't da only one who come to know herself betta. Darcy-boy do da same thang. Fool admit dat he "been a selfish being all [his] life, in practice, though not in principle. . . . By [Lizzy], [he] was properly humbled" (369).

WHAT YOU SEE VS. WHAT YOU GET

Durin' da nineteenth century, men and women sho as hell weren't treated as equals. Lizzy's sista Mary reppin' dat conservative thinkin': dat a woman's gotta keep her shit in line or face gettin' snubbed by society (298).

Thang is, it sometimes hard to tell if Austen playin' us or not. Is she talkin' down 'bout this society? Or no? Maybe she actin' like Lizzy sometimes do—jus' spittin' words she don't believe. Like Darcy say to Lizzy, "You find great enjoyment in occasionally professing opinions which in fact are not your own." (198)

But what do Austen really want us to believe? In a world where men s'posed to be callin' all da shots, Austen show us dat erry now and then, it's da man whose ass is in check:

It is a truth universally acknowledged, that a single man in possession of a good fortune, must be in want of a wife. . . .

He is considered as the rightful property of some one or other of their daughters. (43)

Even tho this book takin' place in a society where women ain't allowed to have property, right here we talkin' 'bout a man bein' da **property of a woman!**

⮌ Images 'n' Symbols ⮌

LIZZY'S TRUCKIN' TO NETHERFIELD

When Lizzy gotta roll ova to Bingley's crib to take care of Jane, da voyage symbolizin' da shit she beast through to be da badass she is, and da badass she become: Lizzy got da joose and da will to slog through all sorts of bullshit in order to do what she thinkin' is right, and can do it solo if she have to (70).

PEMBERLEY

Pemberley is da land of Darcy's fresh digs:

It was a large, handsome, stone building . . . in front, a stream of some natural importance was swelled into greater, but without any artificial appearance. Its banks were neither formal nor falsely adorned. (259)

In a lotta ways, Darcy's sweet crib reppin' da kind of person Darcy be—it's big, it's fine, and it's da realest thang you eva gonna see ("without any artificial appearance"). When Darcy open up and tell Lizzy his feelin's, he keepin' it mad real in da same way: "disguise of every sort is my abhorrence." (213)

✑ Say What? ✑

Classic
When Lizzy hangin' wit' Darcy, and dat fool keep starin' at her:

> [Lizzy] could only imagine however at last, that she drew [Darcy's] notice because there was a something about her more wrong and reprehensible, according to his ideas of right, than in any other person present. The supposition did not pain her. She liked him too little to care for his approbation. (87)

But on da real:

> "Darcy had never been so bewitched by any woman as he was by her." (88)

REMIX
Lizzy assume Darcy thinkin', "Ugh, that girl busted as hell." But on da real, he like, "Daaaamn, girl. Back dat ass up."

✦ ✦ ✦

Classic

When Elizabeth realize dat Darcy ain't jus' a hater, she start warmin' up to him:

> But above all, above respect and esteem, there was a motive within [Lizzy] of good will which could not be overlooked. It was gratitude.—Gratitude, not merely for having once loved her, but for loving her still well enough, to forgive all the petulance and acrimony of her manner in rejecting [Darcy], and all the unjust accusations accompanying her rejection. . . . Such a change in a man of so much pride, excited not only astonishment but gratitude—for to love, ardent love, it must be attributed. (277)

REMIX

LIZZY: "Thanks. Even tho I been treatin' you like shit, you still tryn'a hit it. Respect."

✦ ✦ ✦

Classic

Afta Elizabeth give Bingley props for bein' humble, Darcy jump in and be all like:

> Nothing is more deceitful . . . than the appearance of humility. It is often only carelessness of opinion, and sometimes an indirect boast;—for you are really proud of your defects in writing, because you consider them as proceeding from a rapidity of thought and carelessness of execution, which if not

estimable, you think at least highly interesting. The power of doing any thing with quickness is always much prized by the possessor, and often without any attention to the imperfection of the performance. (85)

REMIX

"Bingley, you humble-braggin' muthafucka."

✦ ✦ ✦

Classic

Afta Lydia run off wit' Wickham, Lizzy damn sure dat Darcy gonna kick her to da curb:

> Had Lydia's marriage been concluded on the most honourable terms, it was not to be supposed that Mr. Darcy would connect himself with a family, where to every other objection would now be added, an alliance and relationship of the nearest kind with the man whom he so justly scorned.
>
> From such a connection she could not wonder that he should shrink. The wish of procuring her regard, which she had assured herself of his feeling in Derbyshire, could not in rational expectation survive such a blow as this. (317)

REMIX

Since Lizzy's sista doin' her own thang and not givin' a fuck, her fam's street cred has gone to shit and Darcy won't ever want her.

✦ ✦ ✦

The Great Gatsby

✦ ✚ ✦

∽ So What's the Deal? ∽

Thinkin' dat stackin' mad grands gonna give you da balla life you always wanted is as American as apple pie. Like da H-Town trap rapper Mike Jones once said: "Back then hos didn't want me, now I'm hot hos all on me."

Likewise—Gatsby thinkin' dat since he got dem swole dolla's now, his back-then hunny Daisy gonna drop her man and git wit' him. Livin' high-balla sound real fly, right? Well dat's one of da reasons this book get all da props it do, and some folk think it got da swagga to be considered da "Great American Novel." Gatsby show us dat jus' cuz you got mad cash-monies don't mean you can relive yo' past, and it sho as hell don't mean you a good person. And Fitzgerald layin' down somethin' even mo' raw: Tryn'a live da American dream can turn yo' life into a nightmare.

❧ Homies ❧

NICK CARRAWAY

An Ivy League white boy, and narrata of da book, who move to West Egg for a lil change of pace. He a pretty chill dude and generally keep his chin up in da face of weak-ass shit he see 'round him. Chill as he is tho, it can be pretty hard to see if he tellin' da truth or if he jus' pump-fakin'.

JAY GATSBY

Da mysterious playboy millionaire who this book name afta. At first, nobody know where he got dat thick paper from. Turn out, he hustlin' da streets slangin' alcohol durin' prohibition. And he been chasin' all dat paper to get his hands on da real prize: dat sweet, sweet ass of Daisy Buchanan he use to tap back in da day. This playa goin' above and way, way beyon' jus' to relive his past.

DAISY BUCHANAN

Nick's cous' (or second cousin once removed . . . but in da hood, all dat shit jus' boil down to "cousin") and Gatsby's back-when biddy. She was s'posed to wait for Gatsby 'til he come back from World War I, but when Tom Buchanan swang into her life flossin' all his cheddar, she like, "Fuck dat, Imma shack up wit' this playa." Even tho she know Tom freakin' wit' otha girls behind her back, she jus' drown da pain wit' fancy drinks and expensive shit.

TOM BUCHANAN

Daisy's hubby who come from summodat **old money**. Basically, he one of dem entitled rich white boys who get to pull Daddy's money outta his ass any time he want. Dude's a dumb, empty chump, and see some skank name Myrtle on da side.

JORDAN BAKER

Daisy's homegirl, who always actin' like she don't give a fuck and got rep for bein' scandalous and a cheat. Afta Daisy introduce her to Nick, they get real close. Real, real close. Naw mean?

GEORGE WILSON

A blue-collar mechanic who actually gotta work to make a livin'. Thang is, his woman, Myrtle, don't want no scrub. Naw, she'd rather get freaky wit' a trust-fund baby while George grindin' away to pay da billz. Afta his wife die, fool get tricked into thinkin' it all Gatsby's fault, and put one in Jay's dome before icin' himself.

MYRTLE WILSON

Georgie-boy's wife who jus' ain't satisfied wit' what her husband pullin', so she scratch dat itch wit' her man-candy, Tom. She ain't got no respect for da fact dat George gotta stay on his hustle erry day to bring home da bread.

❧ What Went Down? ❧

Afta roughin' thru da crazy shit of World War I, Ivy League white boy Nick Carraway decide he gonna set up shop in Long Island and start a new daily grind flippin' bonds. Next door to Nick's new digs is da **pimpin'** crib of Jay Gatsby. Gatsby's pad is so damn fly, you **know** this playa be ridin' da money train. Word on da street be Gatsby always throwin' bangin' parties dat attract all da local VIP. Sho seem like dat playboy livin' da life.

One night, Nick roll ova to his cous' Daisy's spot. Daisy and her hubby, Tom, all like, "Yo, Nick, this fine dame right here name Jordan Baker. Why don't you take a crack at dat ass lata?"

So lata, Nick choppin' game at Jordan all alone when Jordan tell him Tom got a lil somethin' somethin' on da side: a **dime** name Myrtle Wilson.

One day, Tom and Nick go for a ride and drop by a garage run by some po' scrub name George Wilson. Since George ain't able to please his wife, Myrtle, she been dirty-mackin' wit' Tom behind George's back. When Tom and Nick on they lil trip, Tom scoop up Myrtle and take her and Nick to an apartment for some alone time. Myrtle get too schwasted and start runnin' her mouth 'bout Tom's wife, Daisy. Tom

All aboard the money train!!!

all like, "Bitch, don't talk 'bout my wife or I'll pop you in yo' mouth." Girl don't listen, tho. Tom pimp-slap Myrtle so hard dat he break her nose. Party's over, bruh.

SWAG!

Lata dat summer, Nick head over to one of Gatsby's ragin' parties where all da richest bitches in da hood geekin' out over Gatsby's swag. This playboy even got himself a pimpin' yellow Rolls!

As Nick lurkin' round da scene, Gatsby holla at him and be all like, "Yo. Don't I know you from back in da shit?" Apparently, Nick and Gatsby were rollin' in da same clique durin' the war. **Soulja boyz!**

Afta da party, Nick find out from Jordan dat Gatsby got **mad** love for Daisy. Word is they had a lil thang goin' back in da day, but then Gatsby's ass got shipped out to da war, so Daisy married Tom while Gatsby was busy glockin' Germans. Da whole reason Gatsby bought dat phat crib was so he could be close to his back-then hunny love. Erry night, Gatsby chills in da back and look past da water to Daisy's dock, where a green light be shinin' bright.

Now Gatsby want Nick to arrange for him a lil one-on-one wit' Daisy.

So Nick hook 'em up at his crib, and at first . . . shit a lil weird. But afta some time, Daisy and Gatsby stoked to be back in each othas lives. Then Gatsby bring Daisy back to his pad, where she flip shit over his crazy swag.

Wit' all dem grands, Nick know Gatsby could prolly pull any girl he want. Why he want Daisy so bad? Maybe she finer in his head than in reality.

As the summer go on, Daisy and Gatsby start chillin' on da reg. One day, Nick head over to Gatsby's, where he see Tom shootin' da shit wit' G-diddy. Tom start thinkin' there be somethin' 'spicious 'bout Daisy and Gastby.

Soon afta, Tom and Daisy head over to Gatsby's for anotha rager. 'Cept this time, Daisy don't really seem to be feelin' it, and peace out early wit' Tom. Gatsby get all butt-hurt, and Nick see dat Gatsby don't jus' want summa Daisy's sweetness; he want her to drop Tom's ass **and** say dat she never loved him in da first place. But Nick be all like, "Come on, Jeezy. Quit trippin'. You tryn'a relive da past, and it looooong gone." But Gatsby all like, "Bitch, you see deez threads? A rich man can do whateva he damn well please."

Then Daisy, Tom, Gatsby, and Nick all take a trip to town togetha. On they way, they make a stop over at Georgie's garage. George say he know Myrtle been' doin' a lil dick-diddlin' on da side, but he don't know who she been bangin'. So he decide to peace outta da city and head west. Tom's nuts shrivel up inside his pants—"At least he don't know it was **me** gettin' nasty wit' Myrtle."

When they reach da Plaza Hotel, Tom get up in Gatsby's grill and call his ass out for gettin freaky wit' his wife. Gatsby all like, "Look, bitch, yo' woman loves me, not you. Matta fact, she **neva** loved you." Das jus' too much for Daisy tho, and now she all confused. Eventually, she decide to jus' stick wit' dat asshole Tom.

Gatsby and Daisy hop up in Gatsby's fresh yellow whip and head back home. Not long afta, Nick and da rest of da crew headin' back when they peep **Myrtle's dead body layin' in da middle of da road.**

Apparently, Myrtle got real towe up ova some bullshit and **jumped** in front of Gatsby's car while Daisy was drivin'. **Drive-by, muthafucka!** When Nick go to see how Gatsby doin', he find him hidin' in da bushes sayin', "Yo. You gotta go check on Daisy for me, bro. She all wiggin' out afta runnin' over Myrtle."

So Nick pop in they crib and find Tom and Daisy jus' kickin' it like ain't nothin' even happen.

Depressed as shit, Gatsby decide to post up in his pool and marinate on life.

Back in da city, dat fool George thinkin' since it was Gatsby's ride dat killed Myrtle—**Gatsby** gotta be da one was nailin' Myrtle behind his back. So George roll up to Gatsby's crib while he chillin' in da pool, pulls out a 9, and puts one in Gatsby's head. Lights out, G. Then, George turn da piece on himself and add one mo' chalk outline to Gatsby's crib—his own.

When news of Gatsby's death hit da street, all sorta smack talk goin' through da hood. Nick realize dat peeps like Tom and Daisy—dem hood-rich, hollow ones—don't give a shit 'bout nobody or nothin'. Tired of all this crazy drama, Nick decide to get da fuck outta da east side.

✂ Themes 'n' Shit ✂

KEEPIN' IT REAL

It's hard as hell to believe anythin' dat Nick sayin' throughout da book even tho he **claimin'** he keep it realer than errybody else, sayin' dat he one of da only honest bruthas he eva known (64).

But how we s'posed to trust this playa when he always flip-floppin' on how he feel 'bout Gatsby, and relayin' info to us while he shwasted? How we gonna know what really went down? Nick actually tell us dat he "been drunk just twice in [his] life and the second time was that afta'noon, so everything that happened has a dim hazy cast over it." (33)

All da judgments we makin' in this book are made for us by Nick; and dat dude **always** contradictin' himself. For example, Nick like to bitch 'bout errybody bein' so damn careless and not givin' a fuck 'bout nobody. At da end of da book, tho, he drop dat biddy Jordan Baker for no damn reason (186). Do as I say, not as I do, naw mean?

✦ SPARKY'S CLASSROOM ✦

Our boy Nick Carraway is what literary hustlas call an "unreliable narrator." Dude's statements and actions have already shown us dat we prolly shouldn't trust a damn word he sayin'.

TRYN'A RELIVE DA PAST

Gatsby is one sad-ass thug. Even tho he throwin' swank parties and always da talk of da town, he far from happy. Fool got a hole in his heart dat he tryn'a fill wit' shit from his past:

THE PAST IS YOURS

"Can't repeat the past?" he cried incredulously. "Why of course you can!" He looked around him wildly, as if the past were lurking . . . just out of reach of his hand. (116–117)

But no matta how phat yo' pockets be, ain't nobody can relive da past; and da idea dat errything was all good back in da day ain't always true. Sometimes da **idea of the past bein' all dat is jus' in yo' head** (101).

But on da real, da dream in his dome so damn romantic dat reality cain't ever hang wit' it. Fool settin' himself up for some raw disappointment. Truth is, dat's somethin' we all tussle wit', like Nick point out at da end of da novel (189).

NOT GIVING A FUCK

Pretty much nobody in this novel give a damn 'bout nothin'. Tom, Daisy, and all da otha white folk 'cept Gatsby jus' livin' for da moment not givin a shit 'bout anythin' dat last. Narcissists.

They were careless people, Tom and Daisy—they smashed up things and creatures and then retreated back into their money or their vast carelessness or whatever it was that kept them together, and let other people clean up the mess they had made. (187–188)

For example, Daisy is da one who mercs Myrtle, but Gatsby's

da one who gotta ride da beef. Gatsby get capped, and Daisy jus' go on wit' her life like nothin' eva happened.

What make Gatsby so damn great—like da book's title indicatin'—is dat unlike da rest of deez shallow rich folk, Gatsby actually believe in somethin': love, dawg. He build himself a new identity jus' for Daisy. Errybody else straight-up empty inside.

DREAMS AND REALITY

All yo' life you prolly heard dat if you bust yo' ass and stack enough cash, you'll have success and happiness. Mah man Gatsby got all dem thangs, but he sho as fuck ain't happy. Maybe da American dream ain't all it cut out to be.

One symbol of da way dat dreams and reality don't always align in this novel is Gatsby's books. See, Gatsby got all deez books in his library, but he actually jus' flexin'. Dude ain't read none of 'em.

In fact, Gatsby's whole damn life a front. Jay Gatsby ain't even his real name—his mama call him James Gatz (104).

But here's a *paradox* for ya'll hustlaz. On one hand, Gatsby ain't an actual flesh-and-blood brutha. "Gatsby" is a fantasy dat his seventeen-year-old self made up.

But on da otha hand, he da realest homie in da book; he's the only one who love somethin' so damn much he willin' to fight for it.

✦ SPARKY'S CLASSROOM ✦

Paradox: Paradox is a real fancy way of sayin' somethin' dat sound like it contradictory, but actually true.
Example: Tom is da brokest rich dude you eva saw.
Explanation: "Brokest" and "rich dude" don't seem like they

could go togetha; but when you really think 'bout it, we could be sayin' dat even tho Tom's pants saggin' from those Benjamins, he actually po' cuz he bankrupt of morals and love.

❧ Images 'n' Symbols ❧

DA GREEN LIGHT

When Nick first meet da Gat-baby, he always peepin' a green light cross da pond at Daisy's spot. At first, da light remindin' Gatsby dat he close to Daisy—a literal light in da darkness of his life.

But afta Gatsby's heart get shat on, dat light mean somethin' different—it start symbolizin' all Gatsby's dreams and how da world won't let him fo'get da past. Nick start marinatin' on what was goin' on in Gatsby's dome "when he first picked out the green light at the end of Daisy's dock," and he say:

> Gatsby believed in the **green light, the orgastic future that year by year recedes before us.** It eluded us then, but that's no matter—tomorrow we will run faster, stretch out our arms farther. . . . And one fine morning—
>
> So we beat on, boats against the current, borne back ceaselessly into the past. (189)

DAISY A *SIREN*

✦ SPARKY'S CLASSROOM ✦

"Dafuq is a Siren?"

A Siren is a Greek mythological creature who always killin' sailors by singin' sweet tunes, seducin' 'em, and then wreckin' they shit. They were part bird, part woman, and all bidness.

Da ways Nick describin' Daisy associatin' her wit Sirens:

- ✦ "There was an excitement in her voice that men who had cared for her found difficult to forget: a singing compulsion." (14)
- ✦ "I've heard it said that Daisy's murmur was only to make people lean toward her." (13)
- ✦ "That voice held him most, with its fluctuating, feverish warmth, because it couldn't be over-dreamed—that voice was a deathless song." (101)

Like Sirens, Daisy sucks Gatsby in, and cuz of his fiery passion for dat ass, he end up dead.

DA EYES OF T. J. ECKLEBURG

This book always goin' off 'bout images of eyes—'specially da eyes of some pimp name of T. J. Eckleburg. Deez big blue peepers jus' stare out over a wasteland (27).

Now, I haven't da slightest goddamn clue who this Eckleburg thug is, but George Wilson droppin his name cuz he thinkin' dat justice gonna come for dem haterz who livin' empty lives: "God sees everything" (167). But once he try to lay out summodat street justice, he fucks up and end up killin' Gatsby, who be innocent. What a joke, bruh. Maybe da eyes really tellin' us one thang: Dat errything and erryone you countin' on—lovers, friends, God—they all gonna let yo' ass down.

⤙ Shout-Outs! ⤚

Givin' props to otha works dat preachin' da same truths as *The Great Gatsby*.

Classic

I have spread my dreams under your feet;
Tread softly because you tread on my dreams.
    —W. B. Yeats, "He Wishes for the Cloths of Heaven"

REMIX

Yeah, a bullet ends Gatsby's life for sho; but dat ain't what really kill him. Gatsby died cuz he lived in a world where ain't nobody sincere and nobody give a damn 'bout anybody.

✦ ✦ ✦

Classic

I wish you to know that you have been the last dream of my soul. In my degradation I have not been so degraded but that the sight of you with your father, and of this home made such a home by you, has stirred old shadows that I thought had died out of me. . . . I have had unformed ideas of striving afresh, beginning anew, shaking off sloth and sensuality, and fighting out the abandoned fight. A dream, all a dream, that ends in nothing, and leaves the sleeper where he lay down, but I wish you to know that you inspired it.

—Charles Dickens, *A Tale of Two Cities*

REMIX

Gatsby didn't jus' dream of Daisy; he dreamt a **new version of himself** into existence. But when errything said and done, our boy was left wit' jack shit.

✦ ✦ ✦

Classic

Really, what I was writing was just *The Great Gatsby* updated a little. It was "apostolic" fiction—where a surviving apostle tells the story of his hero. There are two men and a woman. And one man, the hero, is shot to death.

—Chuck Palahniuk on writin' *Fight Club*

REMIX

Ain't dat some shit?

Frankenstein;

or,

The Modern Prometheus

✦ ✚ ✦

❧ So What's the Deal? ❧

When *Frankenstein* dropped in da early 1800s, its twenty-year-old author, Mary Shelley, didn't take no credit for it, and da book got published anonymously. 'Bout five years lata, tho, Shelley made sho errybody readin' dat book knew her name. Girl musta' realized Franky was gonna go platinum one day.

And dat girl definitely created a monster. *Frankenstein* dealin wit' all sortsa legit themes: what it mean to be human; whether a creator responsible for what its creation do; and whether we accountable for what we do, or are we jus' a product of our environment?

Like you prolly know, da story of Frankenstein still errywhere: there a shit ton of Frankenstein movies, TV adaptations, fan-fic knockoffs, and even a play.

As man learn mo', innovate mo', and explore da science game further than eva before, *Frankenstein* always there to remind us dat if you try to play God, you gonna pay the goddamned price.

⋙ Homies ⋘

VICTOR FRANKENSTEIN

Vick only got two thangs on his mind: pushin' da limits of science (or what he callin' natural philosophy) and his adopted sista Elizabeth's **sweet, sweet bootay**. Victor take natural philosophy to a whole new level when he create a monster, and then spend most of da book buggin' out. Not only do he feel guilty for bringin' some fugly-ass thang into da worl', but also for causin' a shit storm of pain for his family.

THE MONSTER

Made from a buncha stitched-togetha body parts, Frankenstein's monster is one ugly muthafucka. And if bein' fugly in a shallow-ass world ain't bad enough, worst part is: dude is pretty damn smart; so not only is da world shitty to him, but he know it too. And cuz his creator, Frankenstein, ain't gonna do a damn thang to make his life betta, he gonna get straight monstrous on Frankenstein's ass. Revenge, sucka!

ELIZABETH LAVENZA

Years back, da Frankenstein fam adopted Elizabeth off da streets, and she basically become Vick's lil sista. But dat don't matter none to Victor, who got it **bad** for dat ass. To Victor, Elizabeth stand for errythin good and beautiful in this jacked-up world.

ROBERT WALTON

An explorer who find Victor in his hella fucked-up state up in da Arctic. Jus' 'bout da whole book is a story within a story: Victor tellin' Walton 'bout what the hell happened and why you gotz to watch out when pursuin' knowledge.

HENRY CLERVAL

Victor's main brutha from anotha mutha. They been boys since back in da day, and whenever Victor gettin' sick from all da crazy shit goin' on in his life, Henry be da one who gonna get his back and help a brutha out.

ALPHONSE FRANKENSTEIN

Victor's righteous pops who always lookin' out for his family, even tho' he ain't got da slightest clue what kind of crazy shit his son into.

WILLIAM FRANKENSTEIN

Victor's lil bro who gets straight **merced** by da monster. Coooooold-blooded.

JUSTINE MORITZ

A lil biddy dat da Franken-fam treat like they own. After da monster ice Victor's bro, Willy, he plant some evidence on Justine incriminatin' her, and now she gotta ride da beef for da murda. In da end, she get executed and Victor feelin' **really** shitty 'bout it. Man, sucks to be this girl.

⤜ What Went Down? ⤛

Da beginnin' of this book don't read like a regular story. We checkin' some letters from an explorer named Robert Walton who on his way to da North Pole. As Walton and da crew flowin' down the balls-cold Antarctic, thangs start gettin' a lil trippy: for example, he and his boys spot' a big monster-lookin' thang on a sled.

Lata, they find some bruh lookin' like his shit got **wrecked**. Walton keep him on da boat, heal him up, and asks, "Dafuq, man?" And da guy like, "Aight, aight, I'll tell you my story, yo."

Dat jacked-up fool is Victor Frankenstein. Back when he was a baby thug, da Frankenstein family scooped a lil thugette named Elizabeth, whose real parents long gone. Ever since, Ol' Victor been layin' da mack down and tryn'a avoid dem awkward boner moments.

As da years pass and Victor's balls start low-ridin', he find himself not givin' a shit 'bout nothin' but natural philosophy. At fifteen years ol', Victor see some lightnin' fuck a tree up and all like, "Word. Gonna remember dat."

✦ SPARKY'S CLASSROOM ✦

"Natural philosophy" is what they call science way back in da day.

Lata, some dude chillin' wit' da Frankenstein fam drops some electricity knowledge on Victor, and get our mad-scientist-to-be all confuscd, since it don't jive wit' errything else Victor been readin'.

Two years lata, Victor ready to get his ass to college. No gravity bongs and keg stands for this playboy. Naw, blood. He plannin' to get dat knowledge game **sowed up**. But jus' before he 'bout to jet, his mama up and dies, givin' Victor a lil reminder 'bout how important family is.

Up at school, Victor holla at a prof named Waldman, who get Victor's ass in gear for natural philosophy—'specially chemistry.

Victor get so amped dat he masters all his teachers' knowledge like it ain't **nothin'**. Matter of fact, he show up dem hustlaz by uncoverin' the secret to life. In da process, he get so into his work dat he pretty much fall off da face of da planet.

Combinin' errything he know, and makin' plenty of new discoveries long da way, Victor succeed in creating new life! Thang is, tho, Victor's experiment come out so ugly dat he has to get da hell outta there **ASAP**. Dude passes da fuck out in da next room.

When Victor wake up, he see dat nasty mug all up in his gril, screams like a bitch, and **bails**!

Fool run around town like he lost his damn mind and eventually bump into his old homeboy Henry Clerval. Henry like, "What up, playboy?" They go back to Victor's crib, and Vic see da monster ain't there no mo'. Victor so happy dat he jus' start laughin', but not in da good way . . . Turn out all of Victor's experimentin' dun drove his ass nuts, givin' him a debilitatin' "nervous fever."

Lata, he get a letter from his baby dip, Elizabeth, sayin': "Cous'! Get yo' sick ass back to Geneva." Victor take his sweet time till Daddy Frankenstein send him a letter: turn out Vic's lil bro, William, been **murdered**.

Victor get off his ass and book it to Geneva. Strollin' up to his lil bro's chalk line, Victor see da monster creepin' in da distance and start thinkin', "I made da monster dat merc'ed lil bro William. Ain't dat some shit."

But when Victor get back to da crib, errybody sayin' dat his homegirl **Justine** iced William. See, afta da murda, they found one of William's pictures in Justine's pocket. Eventually, a buncha judges convict Justine of da crime and decide she ain't gonna do no hard time: It's da scaffold for dat girl.

So now Victor **really** all kindsa towe up: Not only did dat monster put his lil bro six feet deep, but he also framed Victor's homegirl. When dem dark thoughts come a knockin', ain't nothin' Victor like more than gettin' some fresh air. He take it outside, start walkin' 'round, and all of sudden see somethin' **big** haulin' ass toward him! Victor realize it's da monster, and like, "Aw, hell naw. **Break yo'self, son!**" But Victor jus' flexin', cuz da monster got at least two hundred pounds on his scrawny self. Da monster laughs at his sorry ass, and then tell him to sit down and listen.

—〰—

Comin' into existence was a **trip** for da monster: He had nobody in da world to feed him, house him, or teach him a damn thang, since Papa Frankenstein is one of dem deadbeat daddys.

Dude so ugly, he cain't even make a single damn friend; errytime somebody see him, they run like hell. But since da monster don't really have anything else to do, he keep tryin'. This time, he shack up next to a lil cottage and peep a nice-lookin' crew.

Afta creepin' on 'em for a lil while, da monster learn 'bout language, history, philosophy, and religion.

One night he roamin' through da woods, where he find somebody's man-purse jus' lyin' in da dirt. Inside, he find a few books: Goethe's *The Sorrows of Young Werther*, a volume of Plutarch's *Lives*, and Milton's *Paradise Lost*. When homebody read *Paradise Lost*, he thinkin' erry word is true.

✦ SPARKY'S CLASSROOM ✦

Milton's *Paradise Lost* is a seventeenth-century classic, talkin' 'bout Satan gettin' his red ass thrown outta heaven and then settin' up shop in hell. It also talk 'bout the creation of man, and all da good shit dat God give 'em before they get booted outta da Garden of Eden.

Prollem is, knowledge almost always come at a price: Da monster find a few of Victor's writings in some threads dat he swiped from Vic, talkin' 'bout how much he hate da monster. If Vic's creation never learned to read, he'd never know how much his own daddy hated him.

Needin' a shoulder to cry on, da monster run up on dat cottage beggin' for friends. When they catch sight of him, tho, they run his lonely ass outta they digs.

Lata, da monster start makin' his way to Geneva. On da way, he see some lil biddy drownin'. Even tho da monster save her, he **still** get attacked by some rando jus' cuz he ugly as hell. Fool even pops a cap in da monster's ass!

Da monster gets betta and runs into Victor's bro, William. Lil Willy talkin' all kindsa mess 'bout da monster's jacked-up mug, and then mentions da name "Frankenstein." Soon as da monster hear dat shit, he decide it goin' down: To take revenge on his creator— Victor—he straight choke a bitch. Then he take Willy's photo of a fine-ass woman and slip it in Justine's pocket while she sleepin'. **Somebody call Johnnie Cochran.**

Afta explainin' all this mess to Victor, da monster like, "You gotz to do me a solid and make me a female monster so I can have some-one to chill wit'." Victor say nah at first, but da monster like, "Look, B, you created me. Any creator worth a shit gonna make sure his creation ain't lonely, amirite? Plus, you do it, you won't ever see me again." So Victor say, "Aight."

Victor leave town and start buildin' dat biddy monster. One night, tho, Victor like, "Hold up . . . if my two creations start bangin', there gonna be a whole race of deez damn thangs. **Nope.** Not happenin' on my watch, chump." So he **destroy** da woman-in-progress while da monster watchin'. Dat monster get **hella pissed** and say all scurry-like, "See you on yo' wedding day, Pops."

Victor get ready to peace outta town, but the po-po get all up in his shit sayin' he under 'spicion for murda. Say whaaaaat? When he see da body, Victor passes the fuck out **again**—da choked-out cat in front of him is Henry Clerval, his main bro.

Victor wake up in da clink and is damn sure dat da monster did this. Wit' da help of his dad, Victor clear his name, get outta lockdown, and make it back home, where he gonna marry Elizabeth.

On his weddin' night, Victor start tweakin' out, rememberin' da monster's promise to see him on his weddin' night. Right before he and Elizabeth 'bout to activate da love machine, he starts lookin' 'round for da monster. While Victor scopin' da scene, he hear Elizabeth scream. Vick's monster jus' claimed one mo' victim, and now Victor know jus' how dat monster feel—alone.

Victor's daddy so damn shocked 'bout all this tragic shit dat he up and die too. Now dat he ain't got nothin' to live for, Victor decide he gonna spend his days tryn'a go **beast mode** on dat monster. Durin' his travels, he meets Walton, tell his story, and then dies.

Walton go back to where Victor's body chillin', and peep da monster hangin' over his dead creator. He say he didn't take no joy sippin' dat evil joose, but now dat his creator dead, he ain't got nothin' to do no mo'. Wit'out a purpose on this planet, he ready to die too. Damn.

⤬ Themes 'n' Shit ⤬

ANGELS 'N' DEMONS

We got a story here 'bout somebody creatin' new life (like God), and then da creation goin' **ham** before throwin' his middle finger up to his creator (like Satan).

Cuz of dat association, there be a lot of biblical language slung up in here to indicate dat **good** characters be all angelic, like Elizabeth's fine self, who "heaven-sent" (20) and got a "saintly soul" (23).

Whereas darker, mo' sinister homies gon' be associated wit' demons and diabolical shit (67). Da monster tell Victor, straight-up: "I ought to be thy Adam; but I am rather the fallen angel" (81).

DEADBEAT DADDIES—UPSTAIRS AND ON EARTH

Victor don't got a damn clue of how dirty he's done his monster. A lotta times dat he talkin' 'bout how good he's had it, he usually sayin' it cuz his parents had dat mommy-daddy game on lock. So when Vick's actin' like a scumbag pop, he only showin' how shitty thangs be for da monster. Victor say, "No human being could have passed a happier childhood than myself. My parents were possessed by the very spirit of kindness and indulgence" (23). But da monster's childhood, tho:

> "I expected this reception," said the demon [the monster]. "All men hate the wretched; how, then, must I be hated, whom am miserable beyond all living things! Yet you, my creator, detest and spurn me, thy creature." (81)

PARADISE LOST—GOD AND ADAM

One of da books da monster find in da woods is John Milton's fresh poem *Paradise Lost*. Shelley already dun told us to peep game at *Paradise Lost* by usin' a quote from it in da epigraph. Now she dun put da damn thang **in** da story.

✦ SPARKY'S CLASSROOM ✦

Da word "epigraph" got ancient Greek roots, and translate to "in front of da writin'." An epigraph is a quote or a chunka text put before a work dat s'posed to give da reada or listna a heads-up 'bout da work's major theme or themes.

Unlike God, who look afta his creation (Adam) like he his own blood, Victor jus' leave Frankenstein out in da cold. Even tho Adam eventually got booted outta the Garden of Eden, he still got a lil taste of paradise. But the monster never got to experience nothin' but a bent-ass world, hatin' on him 24/7.

Da monster ain't only associated wit' Adam, but wit' Satan too. Jus' like Satan, who got beef wit' God afta he booted him outta heaven, da monster gonna rebel against his creator and devote all his time to makin' Victor's life suck. Da monster even say dat "many times I considered Satan as the fitter emblem of my condition" (110).

IT TAKES TWO—THE DOUBLE

It sucks a fat one to be all alone. And ain't nobody know dat pain mo' than da monster, who consider himself "unfashioned" and "half made up" cuz he ain't got nobody to chill with (13).

But he ain't da only one talkin' 'bout da importance of havin' someone else. Walton also talkin' 'bout how he ain't a "whole being" without somebody to coversate wit' (4).

Not only do Frankenstein feel this way 'bout Elizabeth, but da monster reflectin' dat same **humanly** desire when he ask Victor to make him a lady-monster:

> I am alone, and miserable; man will not associate with me; but one as deformed and horrible as myself would not deny herself to me. (123)

Sometimes, Victor even see da monster as part of himself—like it some kind of deranged soulmate. Victor talk 'bout da monster like he po'ed part of his own life-force into it. Maybe dat's why he get sicker and sicker afta da monster born:

> I considered the being whom I had cast among mankind . . . **my own spirit let loose from the grave,** and forced to destroy all that was dear to me. (60)

GET YO' NATURE ON, SON

Even when thangs get **real** shitty, da great outdoors make Victor feel a whole lot betta:

The awful and majestic in nature had indeed always the effect of solemnizing my mind, and causing me to forget the passing cares of life. (79)

What's crazy, tho, is dat da monster say da same damn thang:

My spirits were elevated by the enchanting appearance of nature; the past was blotted from my memory, the present was tranquil, and the future gilded by bright rays of hope and anticipations of joy. (96)

Yep. Creator and creation ain't so different.

TURNS OUT, YOU *CAN* GET TOO HIGH [ON KNOWLEDGE]

Altho most homies would say pursuin' knowledge is righteous, even knowledge has its limits. If taken too far, it can be dangerous as hell. Frankenstein's attempt to take the science game **next-level** end up leavin' a gnarly line of body bags. And he ain't da only character who gets a hard-on from pushin' da limit. Like da explorer Robert Walton say:

How gladly I would sacrifice my fortune, my existence, my every hope, to the furtherance of my enterprise. One man's life or death were but a small price to pay for the acquirement of the knowledge which I sought. (12)

In Greek myth, a lil homie named Icarus was in da pen wit' his pop, Daedalus. Daedalus, one of da baddest inventors in da world, ghetto-rigged some waxen wings so he and his boy could get da hell out. There was jus' one catch: You fly too close to da sun, da wax melts, and yo' ass end up dead. When Icarus ignore his daddy's advice, he find himself in an early grave.

✌ Images 'n' Symbols ✌

THE NEW-SCHOOL PROMETHEUS

Jus' in case you ain't in da know, this book got a subtitle: *The Modern Prometheus*—cuz Victor goin' through some shit similar to Prometheus from Greek myth.

Way back when, Prometheus look down at man and realize how jacked-up peeps' lives be. So to make errything a bit easier, Prometheus decide he gonna bring fire to humanity. Thang is, he gotta swipe it from da gods. When he gank dat heavenly flame, humanity's life got a whole lot betta.

But **his** got a hell of a lot worse. When da Big Daddy of the gods, Zeus, realize what ol' Prometheus up to, he jack dat fool **up**: Prometheus get tied to a rock in da middle of butt-fuckin' nowhere, and a bird swoop down to eat his liver **erryday**.

Da novel got a lot of similarities to dat story, but also be different in some important ways—like Prometheus, Victor think he givin' humanity a gift by creating new life. And to create dat life, he also gotta jack "fire from the sky"—lightnin'.

But instead of makin' a betta world, all he do is bring death and destruction to erryone 'round him. And like Pro-meezy, Victor's life turn to shit cuz he overstep his boundaries.

✌ Say What? ✌

Classic

When Walton writin' his sista and goin' on 'bout how lonely he be:

> But I have one want which I have never yet been able to satisfy, and the absence of the object of which I now feel a most severe evil. I have no friend, Margaret; when I am glowing with the enthusiasm of success, there will be none to participate my joy; if I am assailed by disappointment, no one will endeavor to sustain me in dejection. I shall commit my thoughts to paper, it is true; but that is a poor medium for the communication of feeling. I desire the company of a man who could sympathize with me, whose eyes would reply to mine. (4)

REMIX

WALTON: Errybody needs a bro' to chill and keep it real wit'. For real.

✦ ✦ ✦

Classic

When da monster hit up Victor afta they ain't seen each otha in a minute:

Remember that I am thy creature, I ought to be thy Adam, but I am rather the fallen angel, whom thou drivest from joy for no misdeed. Everywhere I see bliss, from which I alone am irrevocably excluded. I was benevolent and good; misery made me a fiend. Make me happy, and I shall again be virtuous. (81)

REMIX

MONSTER: I act like shit cuz you treat me like shit. Show a playa some love.

Invisible Man

＋ ✦ ✦

∽ So What's the Deal? ∽

Take a look at a few differen' lists wit' da one hundred best English-language novels of all time, and you def gonna see Ralph Ellison's *Invisible Man* pop up a shit-ton. And it wadn't jus' high-ballas like *Time* magazine and da Modern Library givin' this work da mad props: In 1953, Ellison snagged da National Book Award for Fiction too. **Swaaagga!**

Ain't no wonder peeps been hollerin' 'bout this work for years, cuz *Invisible Man* stacked wit' dem deep troubles dat black folk been tusslin' wit' all throughout da twentieth century. Ellison said dat he started off associatin' his narrata wit' dat nameless hustla from Dostoevsky's *Notes from Underground*; but as Ellison kept writin', his boy began findin' his own voice.

Makes sense, too, cuz one of da narrata's main jams in this book is tryn'a make his voice heard—and himself seen—in a loud, racist world. As time go on, tho, he start thinkin' dat bein' unseen one of da most powerful weapons he got.

◠ Homies ◡

NARRATA (IM—INVISIBLE MAN)

First off, we don't ever get this fool's real name—jus' shit like "Jack the Bear" and "Invisible Man." He a young, educated black man who jus' wanna make his way in a society dat always doin' him dirty. Brutha say he invisible cuz nobody who look his way eva see him. He get **real** busted up tryn'a figger out who he really be, and who he wanna become; and it ain't til da end of da novel dat he decide bein' invisible ain't so bad.

DR. BLEDSOE

Da president of da college where da narrata gettin' his learn on. He end up teachin' IM a hell of a lot mo' than books do, and eventually kick his ass right outta school. This playboy got a crazy-ass amount of power and ambition, and would do whateva it take to hang on to it. He tell da narrata somethin' dat piss him off real good: Even if you swingin' one of da biggest dicks on the block, you gotta tell dem crackas what they wanna hear. Then, you can jus' do yo' own damn thang on da DL.

RAS THE EXHORTER/DESTROYER

Ras as hard-core as they come. Brutha don't think peace between blacks and whites ever gonna happen, cuz all white boys wanna do is hold a brutha down. So Ras tryn'a get errybody to get togetha, rep hard dat old-school African heritage, and **take** they freedom—even if it means smackin' 'round whoever get in his way. Ras think da Invisible Man ain't nothin' but da white man's bitch and try to get **real crunk** on his ass at da end of da novel.

BROTHER JACK

Da Brotherhood big-dawg who say his crew lookin' out for da good of da hood. BJ always claimin' da Brotherhood tryn'a help out da oppressed, but it turn out he frontin' jus' like erry otha white dude da Invisible Man meet. This fool's blind in mo' ways than one: he literally got a glass fake eye, is blindly loyal to dat Brotherhood, and he can't see beyond da color of peep's skin.

TOD CLIFTON

A young brutha who got it all: looks, brains, and characta. Clifton start off as a member of da Brotherhood, but chunk deuce for reasons dat don't get explained. Da next time da narrata see him tho, shit gone real cray: ol' TC sellin' Sambo dolls on da street. Not long afta, fool get put six feet deep when the law roll up on him: pop pop, playa.

✐ What Went Down? ✑

This novel start off wit' a lil meet 'n' greet, where we gettin' da lowdown on our narrata from his own perspective. Even tho we gonna learn all sortsa shit 'bout this hustla, there one thang we ain't never gonna find out: his real name!

First thang this G let us know is dat he an invisible man, but not in da ghostly way. Naw, blood. He say he invisible cuz whenever people look at him, they don't see him; instead, they jus' see his "surroundings, themselves, or figments of their imagination" (3).

This playa tellin' us a story on the DL—actually, 'bout as down-low as you can get. Turn out, da narrata chillin' in some digs underground. Our main man spend his time stealin' electricity, listenin' to tunes, and writin' up a storm, preppin' to hit da streets to make this world a betta place. But before he do that, he gonna tell us how the hell he ended up where he did.

When da narrata was an up-and-comin' thug in high school, he got invited by a buncha old white dudes to deliver a speech, where they gonna hook him up wit' some phat stacks for college.

But dem white boys ain't gonna jus' hand over those ends. First, they put da narrata in a ring and make him bang out wit' some otha hustlaz, like some kinda dogfight.

Afta receivin' a grade-A ass-whoopin', our boy deliver his speech and get a briefcase wit' his college scholarship. Dat night, he has a dream dat da scholarship really a piece of paper sayin', "Keep this nigger-boy running" (33). Man, I woulda slapped dat dream.

Up in college, da Invisible Man get asked to drive 'round a trustee of his college—a rich white dude named Mr. Norton. Norton all like, "Yo, Invis. Show me 'round da hood." So IM take him to da mean streets, where black people goin' hard jus' to make ends meet. They chill a while wit' some brutha name Trueblood who go on and on 'bout how he fucked his own daughta. Seriously. Norton get **real** into what he sayin', but then all of sudden start feelin' like hell.

Our narrata take him to a bar call da Golden Day, thinkin' Norton jus' need to get his drank on. Not long afta they get there, a buncha old black vets start a full-on riot. One of dem geezers say he a docta and help get Norton back on his feet afta passin' da fuck out; and before he go, he school Norton and the narrata on what race relations really be like. It ain't good.

When IM make it back to school, he hear da Reverend Homer A. Barbee spittin' some ill rhymes 'bout da college founder. Right afta dat preachin', da college prez, Mr. Bledsoe, gets hyphy on our boy. See, Bledsoe heard all 'bout da shit dat went down wit' IM and Norton, and kicks the narrata's ass right outta school. Before he do, tho, Bledsoe say he gonna hook a brutha up: He give IM a bunch of recommendation letters, sayin' dat they'll score him a job.

But when our boy still cain't find no work, he start wonderin' what da hell goin' on. He get to one of da places where a dude name Emerson run da show, and Emerson's son crack open a letta before droppin' a bomb on our boy: Turn out dat Bledsoe's letters really sayin' dat IM ain't worth a damn—Bledsoe betrayed his black ass. Emerson's son

feel so bad for Inveezy dat he do him a solid and get him a job at a paint factory.

Shit go **ham** when one day at da factory there's a huge explosion and the Invisible Man almost lose his nuts. He wake up in da hospital, where some white doctors doin' electric shock experiments on him, like he some sorta lab rat.

Da narrata get released from dat trap, but he still

That color looks good on you!

PAINT PAINT PAINT

all fucked-up. He's wanderin' 'round da streets til some homies take him to da crib of a biddy name Mary, who help him get betta. While he healin' up, she also learn him good on his black heritage.

One day, da narrata strollin' through da hood of Harlem when he see da law kick a po' black couple outta they crib. IM like, "Fuuuuuck dat," and start gettin' errybody 'round him riled up wit' a speech. Some dude name Brother Jack hear his righteous preachin' and ask him if he wanna join up wit' da Brotherhood—a group of peeps who s'posed to stand up for erryone gettin' fucked by da man. At first, IM ain't really down wit' Jack and his boys. Afta a while tho, he decide to join they gang, since he wanna throw some Benjamins Mary's way for helpin' him out. But as part of provin' he can roll wit' they crew, he gotta change his name, break wit' his past, and chunk deuce to Mary.

Da narrata get tight wit' a young black dude in da Brotherhood name Tod Clifton. He also conversate wit' Ras the Exhorter, who always comin' out way too hard and ragin' 'bout white peeps bein' da enemy, and da Brotherhood bein' a bunch of pussies.

IM keeps movin' up in Harlem and, before you know it, he one of da Brotherhoods big dawgs. When a few members of da so-called Brotherhood start sweatin' IM's growin' power, they kick his ass outta Harlem and give him a new job: fightin' for women's rights.

Dat ain't last long, tho. Shit go south real fast, and da Brotherhood gotta bring IM back. When he return to Harlem, he see dat errything fell apart: Ras da Exhorter got mo' homies at his back, and Tod Clifton up and disappeared. Da narrata eventually find Clifton on da side of da street, sellin' a buncha Sambo dolls.

Since Toddy ain't got no permit, da law get all up in his grill. White cops and a black brutha—this end jus' how it usually do in America: da white cops pump his black-ass full of lead when he wasn't even packin' heat. Michael Brown, Preach!

So da narrata host a funeral for Tod, but Jack and da Bro-hood get all crunk 'bout him doin' it wit'out they say-so.

Lata, Harlem explode into an all-out race riot started by Ras, who rockin' African threadz and throwin' spears at homies. When he see da narrata, he tell his thugz to lynch him.

To make thangs worse, da po-po see da narrata haulin' ass wit' his back-when briefcase and think dat he boosted a buncha shit durin' da riot. So he got da Brotherhood pissed at him; Ras tryn'a stab and hang his ass; and now, some cracka cops tryn'a bust his ass for somethin' he didn't do. While he tryn'a bail, da narrata fall inside a sewer hole and da po-lice shut his ass in there.

And da narrata been down there ever since. Cuz fuck it, this grungy underground crib ain't so much worse than da crooked outside world, naw mean?

But now dat he dun tellin' us his story, he finally feel ready to hit da streets of da upperworld again.

❧ Themes 'n' Shit ❧

INVISIBILITY (DUH)

First off, da invisibility dat da narrata always goin' on 'bout ain't no Harry Potter shit.

Naw. Like our boy say, he's invisible cuz errybody jus' refuses to see him; they only see what around him, themselves, or some idea they imposin' on him (3).

We see what da narrata mean when his young college-self cruisin' round town wit' dat rich-ass bigwig Norton. Instead of Norton recognizin' da narrata as a flesh-'n'-blood human bein', he jus' see him as a cog in his own, mo' important life: "You are my fate, young man . . . my first-hand organizing of human life" (42).

But at first, da narrata actually guilty of not seein' who Norton really is neitha. The vet who help Norton heal up at da Golden Day call both of 'em out on they bullshit, sayin' to Norton: "He believes in you as he believes in the beat of his heart . . . that white is right" (95).

HISTORY 'N' REALITY

History ain't necessarily da truth of what went on back in da day. It's written by da winners, B; and da winners usually da oppressors too. White people got all da power in da novel, and bend da truth to make they **own** reality dat all da otha characters gotta suffer through.

Bledsoe tell da narrata: "These white folk have newspapers, magazines, radios,

spokesmen to get their ideas across. If they want to tell the world a lie, they can tell it so well that it becomes the truth" (143).

In Ellison's novel, they got this shit down to a science. Matta of fact, da narrata don't even eat da damn food he want since white folk would look down on him for it. Poor bastard briefly feels proud for denyin' himself some pork chops and grits (178, 264).

IDENTITY 'N' EXISTENCE

One of da big questions da narrata face is: "Who am I?" Like he say, not knowin' yo'self is like a living death (7).

Our boy spend most of da novel tryn'a figger out who he really be, and feel free as hell when his identity become clear to him (573).

Da narrata ain't da only one who bein' told who he be. Sheeit, dat boy actually do da same thang to Mary. At first, he look at her jus' like Norton looked at him: not as a person, but as a thang. He describe her as: "a force, a stable, familiar force like something out of my past" (258).

As time go on, tho, he start to realize he mighta done dat girl wrong, sayin' "perhaps I had really never seen her" (297).

✍ Images 'n' Symbols ✍

MASKS

Ellison droppin' mask images left and right up in here, and they be
enforcin' da themes of invisibility, reality, and identity. Even tho he
don't realize it as a lil thug, all dem students at Bledsoe's college jus'
bein' who da world tellin' 'em to be:

> The students move with faces frozen in solemn masks, and
> I seem to hear already the voices mechanically raised in the
> songs the visitors loved. (111)

Doc Bledsoe take dat shit next-level. Instead of lettin' somebody
define his identity for him, Bledsoe make his own mask so he can
do what he want on da sly. Before he 'bout to talk wit' Norton,
he jump in front of a mirror and start puttin' his act on: "Bledsoe
stopped and composed his angry face like a sculptor, making it a
bland mask" (102).

But whether you a big dog or an underdog, you gotta watch out
when you rockin' a mask. Like da Invisible Man fine out when he
sportin' specs and a hat, changin' the way you look do jus' as much
on da inside as it do da outside:

> Why am I talking like this? . . . Why am I acting from pride
> when this is not really me? . . . If dark glasses and a white hat
> could blot out my identity so quickly, who actually was who?
> (488, 489, 493)

EYES 'N' BLINDNESS

Peep deez peepers.

Sometimes da narrata cain't see shit: on da figurative, meanin' he cain't see da truth; and on da real, he sometimes **literally** cain't see a damn thang. When high school IM get tricked into tusslin' wit' a buncha bruthas so some old honkies can laugh they asses off, he say dat he ain't got no control or dignity cuz he blindfolded (22).

In this text, not bein' able to see a goddamn thang usually indicatin' how much somebody can see da truth. Homer A. Barbee, da brutha who talkin' up da college founder, is actually blind, which could be Ellison's way of tellin' us dat he cain't see da world for how it really be (133).

> ✦ **SPARKY'S CLASSROOM** ✦
>
> It prolly ain't no coincidence that Homer A. Barbee is a blind dude spittin' some righteous rhymes. This right here prolly a shout-out to one of da most famous peeps who ever lived: Homer. Homer s'posedly lived in ancient Greece 'round da eighth century BCE, and was an epic poet most peeps think be responsible for composin' Europe's oldest literature: the *Iliad* and the *Odyssey*.

Dat OG docta-vet, and da Invisible Man too, usin' images of eyes to talk 'bout truth and bullshit. Da vet tell IM, "for God's sake, learn to look beneath the surface" (153). Lata, when IM givin' a speech in Harlem, he say, "Let's take back our pillaged eyes! Let's reclaim our sight; let's combine and spread our vision" (344).

STATUE OF DAT COLLEGE FOUNDER

Dat statue symbolizin' da themes of blindness, oppression, and not knowin' who you actually servin'. Even tho da founder s'posed to represent good shit like lendin' a brutha a hand, da narrata call him out on dat shit, askin': Is he really helpin' da people he claimin' to? Most bruthas who look at da statue see da founder lifting a veil dat's hangin' over da head of a kneelin' slave. But da narrata ain't so sure dats what's goin on:

> I am . . . unable to decide whether the veil is really being lifted, or lowered more firmly in place; whether I am witness-ing a revelation or a more efficient blinding. (36)

In a lotta ways, dat statue don't jus' represent da founder, or even da narrata's college. Naw, playboy. Dat same image of da founder symbolizin' da Brotherhood too: Even tho they look like da real deal, they really jus' holdin' bruthas back for they own ends.

CATCHIN' Z'S 'N' WAKIN' UP

What you know 'bout images of sleepin' and wakin' up, son?

Ellison pushin' pictures of sleep, dreams, and nightmares to point out who can really see da truth of da world (422).

> NARRATA: "I remember that I am invisible and walk softly so as not to awaken the sleeping ones." (5)

> NARRATA: "All dreamers and sleepwalkers must pay the price." (14)

⌁ Shout-Outs! ⌁

Givin' props to otha works dat preachin' da same truths as *Invisible Man*.

Classic

Dear, dear! How queer everything is to-day! And yesterday things went on just as usual. I wonder if I've changed in the night? Let me think: *was* I the same when I got up this morning? I almost think I can remember feeling a little different. But if I'm not the same, the next question is, "Who in the world am I?" Ah, *that's* the great puzzle!

—Lewis Carroll, *Alice in Wonderland*

REMIX

It take da Invisible Man a while to figger it out, but most of his life spent tryn'a find out who da hell he really be. All throughout his journey, tho, there be all kinda haterz tryn'a break him off and tell him who he gotta be.

✦ ✦ ✦

Classic

Because it is my name! Because I cannot have another in my life! Because I lie and sign myself to lies! Because I am not worth the dust on the feet of them that hang! How may I live without my name? I have given you my soul; leave me my name!

—Arthur Miller, *The Crucible*

REMIX

For a long-ass time, our narrata give up jus' 'bout erry part of himself: how he look, what he act like, what kinda grub he gonna eat, and even what his own damn name is.

✦ ✦ ✦

Classic

> The stares of a million pairs of eyes
> And you'll never realize,
> You can't see me.
>
> —Tupac Shakur, "Can't C Me"

REMIX

At first, da Invisible Man is crushed by da world's inability to see him; dat is, 'til he realize dat invisibility da best weapon he got against a world of haterz.

Lord of the Flies

✦ ✚ ✦

❧ So What's the Deal? ❧

When William Golding's novel *Lord of the Flies* hit da streets of England in 1954, nobody gave a **shit**. Hell, da book went outta print 'bout a year lata. But by da end of da 1950s, Golding's rough rhymes 'bout humanity's dark side got peep's attention; not long afta dat, *LOTF* was as popular as Salinger's *The Catcher in the Rye*.

Not only did Golding win himself a Nobel Prize for **killin'** it at the lit game, but *Lord of the Flies* got dem literary accolades **sowed up**: one of *Time* magazine's 100 Best English-language Novels from 1923 to 2005; one of the Modern Library's 100 Best Novels; and my personal favorite, the American Library Association's list of the 100 Most Frequently Challenged Books of 1990–1999. Word, bitches.

See, not errybody comfortable wit' da way dat Golding uses lil kids to show dat we all got somethin dark lurkin' inside, but far as I'm concerned, recognizin' dat truth is da only way to tame the beast within erryone else. So pick up Golding's monster and get yo' read on, playa play.

✌ Homies ✌

RALPH

Ralph a twelve-year-old British boy and da gang's OG chief. He ain't gotta use muscle to become da leader. He jus' got da swagga dat make people wanna follow him. Ralphie-boy usually got his head screwed on straight, and tryn'a keep errybody in line so they can live in peace. But even tho Ralph got his shit together, he ain't above gettin' a lil cray-cray too.

JACK

One of da oldest boys. Jack in charge of huntin' so dem boys can get their hands on dat meat. Compared to Ralph, Jack a stone-cold gangsta. His trigger finga **always** itchin'. Even tho he got da muscle, he ain't got da mind like Ralph or some of dem otha boys. At first, he too much a sensitive bitch to kill for food. But wit'out society's rules to keep him in line, Jack quickly come to rep the vicious, dog-eat-dog nature of mankind.

PIGGY

He fat, got asthma, and cain't see nothin' wit'out his specs. Pretty much, this lard-ass would be straight useless if it wadn't for his big brain. Even mo' than Ralph, Piggy always actin' as da voice of reason for da whole crew. In fact, he da lil thug who realize dat da conch can be used to call erryone togetha. Piggy reppin' dat civil, intellectual side of humanity. And da fat-ass part.

SIMON

This dude's gotta be da chillest mothafucka on da whole damn island. Errytime I read this book, I'm wonderin' if one of da previous drafts had 'bout ten pages of this fool jus' blazin'. So chill. Dat is, until all da boys fuck him up real good in one big, creepy-ass dance.

ROGER

Jack's right-hand homie, and not somebody you wanna mess wit'. He one sadistic mothafucka.

✌ What Went Down? ✌

Look like humanity dun fucked up again, cuz **anotha** war ragin' through da hood. And speakin' of fuckin' up, a plane full of prissy, proper British boys flyin' ova the Pacific Ocean when—*bam!*—dat hoopty crash-land on an island in da middle of bumfuck nowhere.

When da dust settle, two kids name Ralph and Piggy hop outta da rubble and start scopin' da grounds for otha survivors. See, Piggy got dat name cuz, unlike errybody else, Piggy got a **lotta** junk in da trunk. And dat ain't da only extra pounds he packin': he got way mo' brains than erryone else.

As the boys lurkin' 'round da island, Ralph and Piggy find a white conch shell dat they use to holla at all they boys. Afta hearin' da conch-call, all da kids hook up at da beach.

Otha kids show up at da beach too: a laid-back cat named Simon, a clique of choirboys run by they top dawg Jack, and a group of tiny youngin's who don't know they ass from a hole in da ground.

First order of bidness is to pick a leader. Even tho all dem choir-boys whipped into voting for Jack, errybody else want Ralph to rock da crown. Jack all fired-up 'bout losing the vote, so Ralph say, "Chill, Jackie-boy. You and yo' gang can be whateva y'all want." And Jack like, "Preesh, playboy. We gonna hunt."

As they checkin' what's good 'round da island, da hunter-boys peep a piglet. Even tho it's Jack's job to step up and shank dat ham, he ain't never killed nothin' before. So he chokes like a bitch and da oinker get away. Jack say, "My bad, dawg: next time it ain't gonna be like dat. Dat porker goin' **down**."

Lata, Ralph huddle all da boys to-getha to talk shop. Ralphie lay down da law and say dat ain't nobody got da right to run they mouth unless you holdin' the conch. Gotta have some order up in here, amirite?

When a lil squirt say he peeped a goddamn **beastie** creepin' through da woods, errybody else jus' like, "Shiiiiit, dat boy must be trippin'."

Ralph ain't worried 'bout no monster, and keep sayin' there ain't no such thang. Instead, he focus on organizin' a crew to get they asses rescued. Usin' Piggy's specs, they gonna make a fire so big dat anybody goin' by on a boat or plane would see it. Erryone decide dat Jack and his boys gonna be da ones to make sure dat fire keep burnin'. Since Jack and da choirboys be actin' fools, tho, they almost burn da whole damn forest down.

As time pass, da lil'uns keep havin' trippy nightmares 'bout a beastie. A lil lata, Piggy and Ralph see a ship sailin' by and like, "Oh shit, maybe they'll see da fire burnin' from here . . . wait . . . where's the fire . . . **da fire ain't even burnin'**. Where the fuck is Jack?" Not

LORD OF THE FLIES ◆ 113

long afta, Jack and his crazy crew of choirboys all painted up like savages with a dead pig in tow.

Ralph all like, "**Dafuq, mayne?** You were supposed to keep da fire blazin'." But Jack jus' shake off dat hater and say, "Chill, baby, we got dat meat tho." Ralphie gettin' **real** tired of Jack, and don't understand why errybody ain't more worried 'bout gettin' off da island. Dat fire gotta be numba one, yo.

Ain't long before one of da youngin's start yappin 'bout da monster again. Jack say, "Look, y'all, even if there **is** a monster, I'll put my fuckin' spear right through its ugly-ass mug before it can blink." Then he start messin' wit' Piggy like he always do, and him and his crew run off in da woods screamin' and hollerin' like a buncha wild animals. Any authority Ralph once had pretty much gone to shit.

Lata, there be a big-ass explosion in da sky and a dead parachutist drop from way up high. When a couple of da otha boys catch a real quick peep at dat mangled mess, they run like hell thinkin', "**Oh snap**—it's da monster!"

Afta a few mo' of these lil homies spot da "monster," Jack say dat they gonna need a leader wit' bigger balls than Ralph if they wanna stay safe. So he try to rally da whole crew to give Ralphie da boot, but erryone jus' get real quiet. Jack say he peacin' out, and anyone who wanna join his new crew best follow.

Jack and his new gang of savages kill a sow, rip its head off, and impale it on a stick. When they done, they screamin' all kinda fucked-up shit, like, "Right up her ass!" (135). Yup. Some freaky-ass kids.

Meanwhile Simon jus' wanderin' 'round doin' his own chill thang. He go over and peep dat pig head on a stick, which start **talkin' to him.** Da narrata call dat pig head "the Lord of the Flies." And dat ain't all. Da Lord start spittin' some cold truth up in Simon's ear. It say dem boys ain't got no hope of dodgin' da monster, cuz on da real, da monster ain't nothin' but da violence in da heart of erry human bein'.

While Simon still wanderin' 'round, Piggy and Ralph roll up on Jack's feast where he sittin' highballa. Wit' all dat juicy pork he got, Jack convince most of Ralph's bruthas to drop his scrub-ass and join up wit' his posse. And for afta-dinna entertainment, deez kids say it time to dance. Erryone gather round and start chantin, *"Kill the beast! Cut his throat! Spill his blood!"* (152).

Simon roll up to da party a lil late; and when he do, all deez blood-thirsty kids—even Ralph and Piggy—get so crunk dat they think this fool da beast and murder him in cold blood.

Ralph and Piggy feelin' scurred, confused, and guilty afta dat crazy-ass mess, and thangs ain't gettin' no betta. Ralph's mind keep slippin', and it gettin' harder and harder for him to remember to keep the fire going.

Shit really hit da fan when Jack and his boys run up on Ralph's spot, smack up Ralph and his homies, and boost Piggy's glasses. Not only can Piggy not see a damn thang now, but Ralph and Piggy cain't blaze no mo'.

Ralph ain't havin' none of this bullshit, so he step up to Jack and call him out for swipin' Piggy's specs. Ralph and Jack start tusslin', and then one of Jack's lil cronies slangs a big-ass boulder at Piggy, which smack him right in his grill and make him fall off a cliff. He dead. Like, head-jus'-exploded dead. Ralph book it outta there, and run into the Lord of the Flies while he 'scapin'. When he see dat bacon-y mug, he jus' start swingin' at it, even tho he don't know why.

Jack send his posse afta Ralph, and they decide they gonna smoke him out (but not in da tight way). Eventually, Jack almost burn down da whole damn forest tryn'a find Ralph. As Ralphie haulin' ass, he stumble and fall. When he get back up, he peep a naval officer right in front of him, checkin' to see if erryone aight. Ralph break down into tears, and dem otha little thugs do too.

Yeah, most all dem boys mighta survived, but they far from saved: Afta all dat crazy shit on da island, they innocence is dead.

✌ Themes 'n' Shit ✌

GOOD 'N' EVIL

Way back in da biblical days, Adam and Eve took a bite outta an apple swangin' off da Tree of Knowledge even tho God told 'em they best not. Afta dat, they ain't got no mo' innocence, and get they asses kicked outta da Garden of Eden.

Likewise, Jack was jus' a innocent lil youngin' before he sliced up dat first pig. But afta he get a taste of what it like to be at da top of da food chain, he see a brand-new side of himself—a real dark one . . . and boy do it taste goooood. Afta bustin' his savagery-cherry, Jack don't think twice before gettin' crunk on any fool dat step to him. For Jack, dat pig actin' like Adam and Eve's apple, grantin' him knowledge he didn't have before: "knowledge that they had outwitted a living thing, imposed their will upon it, taken away its life like a long satisfying drink" (70).

Even tho mankind always scurred 'bout thangs doin' 'em harm—creatures, monsters, darkness, the po-lice—truth is, da realest beast comes from within humanity itself. My boy Simon saw dat shit while errybody else wuz jus' sittin' there wit' they thumb up they asses:

> "Maybe there is a beast. . . . maybe it's only us." . . . Simon became inarticulate in his effort to express mankind's essential illness. (89)

CIVILIZED LIVIN' VS. SAVAGE LIVIN'

Society like a big dam holdin' back all humanity's evil tendencies.

But erry time da dam (society's rules) start crackin', all dat anarchy, chaos, and savagery come seepin' in. Cuz on da real, there ain't no wall tough enough to keep all dat mess at bay. Das why Piggy wonderin' what da hell make er-rything go to shit (139).

See, Ralph reppin' da attempt to build a civilization dat gonna keep errything chill between da people. Piggy da brains of da operation, actin' as Ralphy's voice of reason. Dat boy Jack, tho, all insane in da membrane—chaos and killin' in da body of a kid.

WHAT YOU SEE VS. WHAT IS

Civilization ain't nothin' but a mask dat humanity wear to hide da beast wit'in.

But actually, dem masks can be pretty damn useful in keepin' dat darkness at bay. When Jack paint his face, he ges rid of his "civilized" mask and can now do whateva his beastly side feel like. Now he ain't got none of dem man-made rules holdin' him down:

> Jack planned his new face. . . . The mask was a thing on its own, behind which Jack hid, liberated from shame and self-consciousness. (63–64)

But Jack ain't da only one recognizin' what da paint do: Ralph and Piggy get it too, understandin' dat somethin' simple as paint can transform ya into a whole new person (172).

It's pretty damn ironic dat once da kids put on da face paint (a kinda mask), they really takin' off they "civilized" mask. Ya feel me?

This go way beyond jus' what somebody look like. We always makin' assumptions 'bout what we see and thinkin' we know what's what. Truth is, it all boil down to perspective and context. Thangs—and people—change when you put em somewhere else . . . somethin' dem boys learn all too well on da island. Ralph start to understand dat when he gearin' up for a late-night assembly:

> Now . . . , the shadows were where they ought to be. . . . If faces were different when lit from above or below—what was a face? What was anything? (78)

And followin' dat line of thought, a brutha's gotta ask (jus' like this book do): What's a law, 'cept anotha arbitrary construct of man?

❦ Images 'n' Symbols ❦

PIGGY 'N' HIS DOPE SPECS

Piggy and his glasses reppin' da intellect, reason, and logic of civilized livin'. Unlike da rest of dem kidz who grow into hard-core savages, Piggy pretty much stay da same—civil and chill. Dat's why he da only one on da island whose hair don't grow (64).

At first, Piggy's glasses actin' as a symbol tellin' da reader shit gettin' less and less civilized up on dat island. Basically, they like a barometer dat tell how fucked up thangs gettin', at one point flashin' (24) and at anotha point mistin' over (25) afta his bitch-ass get dissed.

Dem shades also symbolizin' civilization itself, cuz through 'em, da kidz able to get fire, warmth, food—all dat legit hood shit. As da book progressin', da glasses get mo' and mo' nastified, showin' da fall of civilized livin'. And once they get stolen, shit's gone straight savage up in here.

They also symbolizin' knowledge. Like my man Prometheus know betta than anyone, knowledge and fire go hand in hand, jus' like dat Promethean Fire, **naw mean**?

FUCKED

CHILL

State of Affairs
on the Island

PIG HEAD ON A STICK

On one level, da Lord of the Flies ain't nothin' more than a lady-pig's head on a stick. But if you wanna take dat lit game next-level, you know it reppin' somethin' far mo' sinister: da darkness dat lie inside erry homie. Da Lord of the Flies is dat thang inside us dat make us steal from the weak, force people to do thangs they don't wanna, and short someone on a dime bag. Da Lord of the Flies say to Simon:

> "Fancy thinking the Beast was something you could hunt and kill! . . . You knew, didn't you? I'm part of you?" (143)

Da name Lord of the Flies is a translation of da Hebrew name Beelzebub, which is anotha name for da **devil**. Cuz like da devil be doin', dat head reppin' all da decay, destruction, chaos, and panic inside erry human being.

Some otha homies suggestin' dat da Lord of the Flies reppin' the Id, or as my coke-bingin' homeboy Sigmund Freud be sayin', da part of us dat only worried 'bout survival.

Even tho they intendin' for da pig head to be a sacrifice to da beast, it's actually a metaphorical sacrifice to da **real** beasty up in here—da one in da heart of erry man.

Tell me about your mother.

DAT CONCH

Da conch shell symbolizin' man's attempt to keep shit orderly. When Ralph and Piggy find this bad boy, they use it to gather errybody together, start a meetin', and decide who got da right to do da yappin'. Crazy thang is, you don't even have to **use** da conch for it to have power ova othas; you jus' gotta hold it. Ralph gets marked as leader cuz of "his size, and attractive appearance; and most obscurely, yet most powerfully, there was the conch" (22).

As life on da island gets mo' raw, da conch start to mean less and less. When it break, Piggy, da reason-slanger, is killed shortly afta. Any hope of peace literally shatters.

BLOWIN' SMOKE 'N' BLAZIN'

On one hand, fire symbolizin' mankind's primal side—cuz it's one of those thangs you need for basic survival. But dat bonfire also givin' dem boys a chance of gettin' rescued, so it also connectin' dem to da outside, civilized world.

Ralphie always gettin' on errybody's ass remindin' 'em dat ain't nothin' mo' important than keepin dat fire blazin'. This reppin' da fact dat he still holdin' on tight to his civilized self. But as time fly by, even mah boy Ralphie start slippin' into savagery. By da end, he can't even remember why dat fire need to keep ragin' (173).

TRIPPIN' 'N' FALLIN'

There be an ass-load of fallin' goin' down in this book. Homies be fallin' metaphorically (like man's fall from grace afta gettin' booted outta da Garden of Eden); and literal falls dat rep da same idea. For example, dat soulja boy parachutin' actually fell outta da damn sky.

But hold up—there be a whole buncha otha falls preachin' dat same idea—Piggy fallin' to his death, da conch shatterin' from da same scrap, Ralph's fallin' at da feet of da naval dude, and da fall of da boys' innocence:

> Simon was dead—and Jack had . . . The tears began to flow and sobs shook him. He gave himself up to them now for the first time on the island; great, shuddering spasms of grief that seemed to wrench his whole body. . . . With filthy body, matted hair, and unwiped nose, Ralph wept for the end of innocence, the darkness of man's heart, and the **fall** through the air of the true, wise friend called Piggy. (202)

∾ Shout-Outs! ∾

Givin' props to otha works dat preachin' da same truths as *Lord of the Flies*.

Classic

But the wilderness had found him out early, and had taken on him a terrible vengeance for the fantastic invasion. I think it had whispered to him things about himself which he did not know, things of which he had no conception till he took counsel with this great solitude—and the whisper had proved irresistibly fascinating. It echoed loudly within him because he was hollowed at the core.

—Joseph Conrad, *Heart of Darkness*

REMIX

When dem lil shits hit da island, they pretty damn sure they jus' reached paradise: a spot where no one gon' tell 'em what to do. All dem noble ideas of civility and decency turn out to be jus' as hollow as deez kids' **real, savage** moral code.

✦ ✦ ✦

Classic

Here comes a raging rush of people, with torches, and an awful whooping and yelling, and banging tin pans and blowing horns; and we jumped to one side to let them go by; and as they went by, I see they had the king and the duke astraddle of a rail—that is, I knowed it *was* the king and the duke, though they was all over tar and feathers, and didn't look like nothing in the world that was human—just looked like a couple of monstrous big soldier-plumes. Well, it made me sick to see it; and I was sorry for them poor pitiful rascals, it seemed like I couldn't ever feel any hardness against them any more in the world. It was a dreadful thing to see. Human beings *can* be awful cruel to one another.

—Mark Twain, *Adventures of Huckleberry Finn*

REMIX

There's a special cruelty dat human bein's always slangin' at each otha, and *Lord of the Flies* show us dat it's somethin' we all got inside us, regardless of age or anythin' else.

✦ ✦ ✦

Classic

> Bitch, I'm a monster, no good bloodsucker,
> Fat motherfucker, now look who's in trouble.
> —Rick Ross in Kanye West, "Monster"

REMIX

Rick Ross musta been talkin' 'bout Piggy's fat-ass here. Amirite?

✦ ✚ ✦

Moby-Dick

✦ ✚ ✦

So What's the Deal?

Errybody know da story of Captain Ahab tryn'a throw down wit' a white whale name Moby Dick. But das jus' da surface level, padna. This book got a whole lot mo' shit goin' on than jus' a buncha homies chasin' a fish. Melville droppin' rhymes 'bout class structures, race, good and evil. Sheeeiit, he also spittin' some righteous philosophical ponderin's through da symbol of dat whale. Mo-deezy ain't jus' a fat-ass fish, he also representin' da pain, indifference, and unknown mess goin' down in this crazy-ass universe. And like Ahab and errybody else in Herman Melville's book, we jus' a buncha sailors flowin' along a big, empty ocean, searchin' for meanin'.

❧ Homies ❧

ISHMAEL

Da book's narrata who barely do a goddamn thang. All he do is talk up mah boy Ahab and go on and on 'bout whalin' bullshit. Still, he da only member of da *Pequod*'s crew dat ain't sleepin' wit' da fishes when errything said and done.

QUEEQUEG

Ishmael's homeboy numba one and a harpooner on da *Pequod*. Queequeg tatted up from head to toe and 'bout as different from Ishmael as can be. But even tho Ishmael and othas first thinkin' Queequeg jus' a gnarly gangbanger, fool is actually pretty damn nice.

CAPTAIN AHAB

Da baddest mothafucka dat ever sailed da seven seas. Fool only got one thang on his mind: findin' Moby Dick, da whale dat took his leg, and makin' him his bitch. He don't give a fuck 'bout nothin' else. Monomania, ya heard?

MOBY DICK

Da legendary white whale dat pulled a real bitch move when he took Ahab's leg. He a big-ass fish and a big-ass mystery, meanin' a hundred different thangs to a hundred different people.

✑ What Went Down? ✑

It all start when this brutha callin' himself Ishmael decide he need a lil change of pace in his life. He wanna get in on dat whalin' grind, cuz erry now and then, he get a little too "grim about the mouth" (27). And ain't nothin' gonna fix this fool like gettin' up on a boat and shankin' some whales. Word.

Ishmael head over to an inn where he meet a harpooner name Queequeg, who all inked up wit' sweet tats. Apparently, there ain't much room in da hotel, so instead of takin' da floor, couch, or a cot, Queequeg and Ishmael decide to share a bed togetha like they Bert and Ernie or somethin'. Even tho Melville don't explicitly say it, there may have been some harpoonin' goin' on in dat bed, if ya know what I'm sayin'.

Queequeq and Ishamel decide they gonna roll bro deep and crew up on a whalin' boat togetha. So they take a trip to Nantucket and hop on a boat call da *Pequod*, which all iced up wit' whale teeth and bones. It's pretty fuckin' tight. Word is, da brutha who runnin' this show is some badass mutha name Ahab who got in a scuffle wit' a whale and lost his leg.

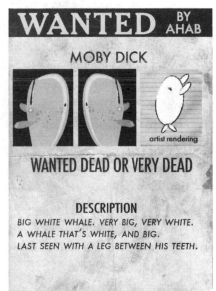

Afta they hit da waves, Ahab eventually roll up to da deck swingin' a dick big enough to make Moby blush. He take a look at da crew and like,

"Look, if y'all don't know what this is, listen up. We got only one mission: to track down Moby Dick, da white whale dat took mah leg, and straight merc dat blubbery fuck. I know you down—right?" 'Course they is. So erryone start throwin' back dat joose and swearin' they gonna **end** dat big-ass whale.

As da crew lurkin' through da ocean looking' for this chubby chump, they tryn'a kill otha whales and pretty much nothin' important happens—Melville jus' give us a shit-ton of info 'bout da life and science of whalin, along wit' stories 'bout legendary whalers.

MOBY DICK BY THE NUMBERS

30% Plot

70% Whaling Bullshit

While da *Pequod* cruisin' down dat watery hood, they hook up wit' one boat (da *Jeroboam*) carryin' some thug claimin' he a prophet. Dat brutha like, "Don't go afta Moby Dick, man. Anyone who go afta dat fat-ass whale gonna get they shit wrecked." But Ahab don't give a **fuck**. Not even death gonna keep him from gittin' dat sucka.

Lata, da *Pequod* roll up on a ship called da *Samuel Enderby* and they top dawg, Captain Boomer. Apparently, Big Boom had a run-in wit' Moby Dick too; and Moby took his goddamn arm off! Thang is, he ain't all bent outta shape 'bout it like Ahab be. He see Ahab talkin' major smack 'bout dat whale and he all like, "Chill, B. Shit happens." Plus, he got a swag new hammer-arm outta it (505).

Lata, Queequeg get sick and they build a coffin for his death. But then, fool get betta and da carpenter like, "Man, r u shitting me? I jus' did dat for nothin'?" But, they end up findin' a new use for it: life buoy. Yup. Coffin as a life buoy.

Time pass, and Ahab get crazier and crazier 'bout findin' dat scrub-ass whale. He so geeked 'bout it dat he get a new harpoon made, and actually baptize it in pagan blood; cuz ya **know** Ahab into dat freaky shit.

As da *Pequod* keep cruisin' along, they conversate wit' da homies of a boat called da *Rachel*. Da captain ask Ahab if he'll do a brutha a solid and help look for his lost son. But Ahab ain't got da time to deal wit' stupid shit like helpin' people find they lost loved ones. He only got one thang on his mind: dat Mo-Deezy.

Finally, Ahab spot Moby Dick chillin' in da water: it's on, blood. Da *Pequod* chase his fat ass for three damn days; but on day three, it's lights out for da *Pequod*'s crew. Moby sinks da *Pequod*, and when Ahab try to go toe-to-toe wit' him, Ahab get pulled underwater by a harpoon line and sink to his death. Errybody end up buried at sea, 'cept one thug: Ishmael, who stay alive by floatin' on Queequeg's coffin. For a whole day and night, dude is jus' floatin' along in da middle of da water, until his lucky-ass get scooped up by da badass bruthas of da *Rachel*. Hallelujah!

✎ Themes 'n' Shit ✎

FATE 'N' FREEDOM

One theme dat always poppin' up is da question: "Is man responsible for his own destiny?"

Melville goin' on 'bout fate, free will, and chance all up in this bitch. Even in da very first chapter, Ishmael say da whole story he 'bout to lay on us is like a big play put on by da Fates, who actin' like they stage managers (32).

✦ **SPARKY'S CLASSROOM** ✦

In ancient Greek mythology, da Fates, or Moirae, were three sistas packin' a shit-ton of power—in some mythological traditions, even mo' than da king a da gods, Zeus himself. They named Klotho, Lachesis, and Atropos, and each responsible for a different slice of a homeboy's life. Klotho weave someone's fated thread, Lachesis assigned dat thread to a particular person, and Atropos sever da thread when it was time for dat same person to die.

Ishmael also talk 'bout dem three Fates when describin' Ahab's blinged-out devil harpoon:

This done, pole, iron, and rope—like the Three Fates—remained inseparable, and Ahab moodily stalked away with the weapon. (563)

For a while, even Captain Badass himself, Ahab, ain't so sho who or what to blame for all da crazy shit dat go down in da world. Hell, when Ahab lift his arm in chapter 132, he even ask if it's God controllin' dat arm or himself (622): "I am the Fates' lieutenant; I act under orders" (641).

PRIDE BEFORE THE FALL, SON

There's a booty-load of tragic elements in this here text. And one of da most old-school is dat a playa wit' a fat head gonna get his ass put in check by da man upstairs—'specially when you spittin' right in his face. Ahab can only talk so much shit 'bout da Big G before his gangsta-ass gets a smitin'.

> I now prophesy that I will dismember my dismemberer. Now, then, be the prophet and the fulfiller one. That's more than ye, ye great gods, ever were. (208)

Ahab's cocky-ass self not only take him and his ride down, but damn-near his whole crew too! Da only brutha dat make it out alive is Ishmael, cuz he know how to **actually** keep it gangsta.

> I abandon the glory and distinction of such offices. . . . I abominate all honorable respectable toils, trials, and tribulations of every kind whatsoever. It is quite as much as I can do to take care of myself. . . . No, when I go to sea, I go as a simple sailor, right before the mast. (30)

In otha words:

> But real gangsta-ass niggaz don't flex nuts
> Cuz real gangsta-ass niggaz know they got 'em.
> — Geto Boys, "Damn It Feels Good to Be a Gangsta"

Unlike Ahab, Ishmael don't give a fuck 'bout pride, glory, and payin' back some asshole who dissed ya; instead, he jus' go wit' da flow. Haterz gonna hate, amirite?

ROLLIN' SOLO VS. HAVIN' A CREW

One of da reasons our boy Ishmael decide to change his hustle and thug it up as a whaler is cuz his mind start slippin'. Brutha start

thinkin' 'bout wreckin' otha people's shit for no reason, and even endin' his life for good. Afta Ishamel meet Queequeg, tho, he realize dat all he needed was a lil brutha-love: "I began to be sensible of strange feelings. I felt a melting in me. . . . This soothing savage had redeemed it" (81).

The novel also sayin' dat whateva one person do can surriously affect otha people too. For example, when Ishmael and Queequeg using dat monkey rope, Ishmael start runnin' his mouth 'bout how erryone in da world is connected. Whateva happen to one brutha gonna affect anotha (376).

But Ahab don't give a **damn** 'bout how his actions affect otha peoples, cuz da **only** thang he givin' fucks 'bout is killin' dat pasty whale. Not only do this fool turn his back on helpin' da *Rachel* search for a lost member of they blood, but he also send his whole damn crew to they death.

When Moby sink Captain Ahab's ride at da end, Big Whitey cut Ahab off from da last bit of community he coulda had:

Death-glorious ship! must ye then perish, and without me? Am I cut off from the last fond pride of meanest shipwrecked captains? Oh, lonely death on lonely life! (652)

ACCEPTIN' PEOPLE OF DIFFERENCE

This book real ahead of its time. Before da Doc King, before Mandela, and before Oprah, ol' Melville talkin' big game on how errybody should be treated equal no matta where you come from, what you look like, or what God you prayin' to. When Ishmael first check Queequeg and all his jail-house-lookin' tats, brutha start buggin': "I confess I was now as much afraid of him as if it was the devil himself who had thus broken into my room at the dead of night" (48).

But soon enough, Ishamel see dat Queequeg is jus' a flesh-and-blood homie like anybody else: "The man's a human being just as I am: he has just as much reason to fear me as I have to be afraid of him" (50).

Fool even step up and start preachin' to othas dat Queequeg got da same right to ride on da *Pequod* as anybody else, cuz we all part of da same community: da human race (121).

✌ Images 'n' Symbols ✌

DA UNKNOWN

+ Ishmael always talkin' 'bout how stupefied people be by unknown thangs in life, and lay it on thick dat shit you can't pin down usually da tightest—Ahab, da sea, Moby Dick, and da whole universe: "For what are the comprehensible terrors of man compared with the interlinked terrors and wonders of God!" (143)

✦ "But that same image, we ourselves see in all rivers and oceans. It is the image of the ungraspable phantom of life; and this is the key to it all." (29)

Maybe dat's one of da reasons Ahab's crazy ass so damn obsessed wit' Moby Dick—cuz dat big-ass whale is jus' one giant mystery.

ORPHANS

Deez images ain't got nothin' to do wit' real mamas and papas. Naw, this book talkin' 'bout a **bigger** deadbeat father.

Whether there actually a God or not, he ain't never comin' around to help his kids out. So on da real, we all orphaned while we live on this earth.

Our souls are like those orphans whose unwedded mothers die in bearing them; the secret of our paternity lies in their grave, and we must there to learn it. (565)

There ain't no spot dat highlight this idea betta than da end of da novel. Da *Rachel*, a ship whose captain searchin' for his lost son, find a different orphan entirely: Ishmael, the only survivor of da *Pequod* (655).

FLAME AND DAMNATION

Images of flame blazin' all through-out this fat-ass book, 'specially when talkin' 'bout Captain Ahab—further connectin' him wit' Christian mythology's Satan (158).

Ahab often wake up in da middle of da night, cuz fool got so much fury ragin' inside dat it like he carryin' round his own personal hell:

> These spiritual throes in him heaved his being up from its base, and a chasm seemed opening in him, from which forked flames and lightnings shot up. . . . This hell in himself yawned beneath him. (245)

Brutha shoulda taken some NyQuil.

AHAB'S NAME

Ahab got power—ain't no question 'bout dat. But even if he like a king in dat way, he sho as hell ain't a righteous one. Matta of fact, da name Ahab is a throwback to a biblical king notorious for doin' wicked shit. When Ishmael cruisin' 'round lookin' for Captain Ahab, he hear dat Ahab's "above the common." Dude even add:

"*He's Ahab*, boy, and Ahab of old, thou knowest, was a crowned king!"

Ishmael, who ain't impressed, fire back, "And a very vile one. When that wicked king was slain, the dogs, did they not lick his blood?" (112–113)

AHAB'S JANKY-ASS LEG

Ahab, even tho he alive, become so obsessed wit' da thought of wreckin' Mo-Dicky dat it's like he both livin' **and** dead—symbolized through his two legs:

> While his one live leg made lively echoes along the deck, every stroke of his dead limb sounded like a coffin-top. On life and death this old man walked. (279)

Dat whale fucked up his head so raw, it's even become a part of his physical body. Sheeeiit, dat whale even give Ahab support—cuz gettin' his revenge on dat whale give him a purpose in life. Without it, Ahab couldn't **stand** to live.

MOBY DICK

Moby Dick mean different thangs to different crew members, but for Ahab, he reppin' all kinda shit. To Ahab, Moby sometimes representin' all da unknown thangs in this world (203).

Otha' times, Mo-deezy reppin all da fucked-up shit 'bout humanity—all da evil and frustrations inside us and out:

> The White Whale swam before him as the monomaniac incarnation of all those malicious agencies which some deep men

feel eating in them. . . . That intangible malignity which has been from the beginning. . . . All evil, to crazy Ahab, were visibly personified, and made practically assailable in Moby Dick. (226)

And otha times, Moby reppin' God himself. Ahab ain't buckin' a whack society, he buckin' a whack **existence**. And whether it be da universe, the sun, God,

or yo mama, Ahab gonna step up and rebel against it 'til he dead. And if dat ain't da most gangsta shit you eva heard, you ain't been listenin'.

DA WHALE'S WHITENESS

Ishmael say there ain't nothin' he hate mo' 'bout Moby than his color. I don't know how dat ain't racist, but whateva. He go on by talkin' 'bout otha terrifyin' thangs dat are white:

The one visible quality in the aspect of the dead which most appals the gazer, is the marble pallor lingering there. . . . All ghosts rising in a milk-white fog. . . . Let us add, that even the king of terrors . . . rides on his pallid horse. (234)

Then, Ishamel go on to say dat mankind so 'fraid of da color white cuz it both **no** color and **all** color. It "stabs us from behind with the thought of annihilation," and at da same time "is a dumb blankness, full of meaning" (238). Creepy.

❧ Say What? ❧

Classic

When Ishmael sit down for dinner, he sees a youngin' who brought his A-game:

> One young fellow in a green box coat, addressed himself to these dumplings in a most direful manner. (40)

REMIX

This playa gettin' his grub on.

✦ ✦ ✦

Classic

Man . . . I don't even know:

> Squeeze! squeeze! squeeze! all the morning long; I squeezed that sperm till I myself almost melted into it; I squeezed that sperm till a strange sort of insanity came over me; and I found myself unwittingly squeezing my co-labourers' hands in it, mistaking their hands for the gentle globules. Such an abounding, affectionate, friendly, loving feeling did this avocation beget; that at last I was continually squeezing their hands, and looking up into their eyes sentimentally. . . . Come; let us squeeze hands all round; nay, let us all squeeze ourselves into each other; let

us squeeze ourselves universally into the very milk and sperm of kindness. Would that I could keep squeezing that sperm forever! (484)

✦ ✦ ✦

Classic

Stubbs givin' Ahab mad props:

> And damn me, Ahab, but thou actest right; live in the game, and die in it! (575)

REMIX

Live by the game, die by the game.

✦ ✦ ✦

Classic

When Ishmael cogitatin' on what it mean by a true-blue gangsta:

> Nor will it all detract from him, dramatically regarded, if either by birth or other circumstances, he have what seems a half willful over-ruling morbidness at the bottom of his nature. For all men tragically great are made so through a certain morbidness. Be sure of this, O young ambition, all mortal greatness is but disease. (106-7)

REMIX

Gotta stay up on yo' grind to be great, and ain't nothin' mo' ill.

✦ ✦ ✦

Classic

When Ishmael yappin' 'bout Starbuck, Ahab's right-hand man, and start thinkin' 'bout what folk really capable of:

> Men may seem detestable as joint-stock companies and na-
> tions; knaves, fools, and murderers there may be; men may
> have mean and meagre faces; but man, in the ideal, is so noble
> and so sparkling, such a grand and glowing creature, that over
> any ignominious blemish in him all his fellows should run to
> throw their costliest robes. (150)

REMIX

Though a lotta peeps sho do suck, mankind got the ability for great-
ness too.

A Raisin in the Sun

✦ ✝ ✦

✑ So What's the Deal? ✑

Lorraine Hansberry's *A Raisin in the Sun* one of da most throwed-up plays you ever gonna read, and true-blue gangstas been givin' it props since it hit da stage in 1959. Hell, even Sean "P. Diddy" Combs wanted a piece of da action, playin' da part of Walter in a 2008 version of da play.

This play don't hold nothin' back and take on some of da biggest issues dat black folk had to beef wit' back in da day: family values, gettin' shit on by da man, establishin' yo' own identity, and most important—what happen when yo' game get so tripped up dat you can't realize yo' life's dreams.

Raisin didn't jus' tap into thangs dat people were gonna go ham over and den forget 'bout. This shit **still** as real as it get, cuz **even today** black people gotta grind through all dat bullshit on da reg. Hopefully, takin' a peep at this play gonna remind you dat da American dream is for **errybody,** and we all deserve an equal shot.

❧ Homies ❧

WALTER YOUNGER

Da man of da family. Even tho he top dawg of da household, he always feelin' like a lil bitch since his job as a limo driver ain't givin' him nuff cheddar to support da family. He think he can make some phat grands by investin' his dead daddy's money in a liqua store, and don't give a damn dat it ain't his call to make. Even tho Walter spend most of da play strugglin' to embrace who he be, and where he come from, he step up at da end, loud and proud.

BENEATHA YOUNGER

Walter's sista who mad educated and always marinatin' on what it mean to be a black girl up in 1950s America. Her milkshake bringin' all da boys to da yard: rich bruthas, intellectual bruthas, you name it. They all tryn'a get a piece of dat Younger ass. Prollem is, they so busy hollerin' dat they ain't payin' attention to Beneatha's own voice.

MAMA—LENA YOUNGER

Walter's mama. She got dat holy spirit flowin' through her. Not only is Mama always sippin' dat Jesus joose, but she got da biggest balls of da family. She ain't afraid to call Walter out on his bullshit dream of makin' money sellin' booze. Mama's main jam is makin' a betta future for her grandson, Travis, and step one: buyin' da family a sweet new crib.

RUTH YOUNGER

Walter's wife, who always tryn'a get erryone to chill whenever da family start gettin' in each otha's grills. There be some tension in the marriage since Walter always feelin' like a scrub. Ruth want nothin' mo' than for da family to get outta they tiny-ass apartment, 'specially since she got anotha baby on da way.

TRAVIS YOUNGER

Ruth and Walter's son. When Walter 'bout to shit on da family pride at da end, takin' a glance at his boy T-Money give Walter da strength to buck up.

JOSEPH ASAGAI

A street smart, book-smart African student who got da hots for Beneatha. He always preachin' to her 'bout reppin' African heritage instead of sellin' out by jus' assimilatin' into white culture.

GEORGE MURCHISON

Rich black playa who also mackin' on Beneatha. 'Cept he like da opposite of Joey Asagai, cuz George basically act like he white. He don't give a shit 'bout da plight of black folk. All he want is a woman dat gonna stay fine and help him count his money.

KARL LINDER

Jive-ass white boy who part of da Clybourne Park Improvement Association—basically da racist version of da Home Owners' Association. He offer to throw some dough at da Youngers to keep they asses outta his hood, but get his ass shut down when Walter tell him where to stick dat dough.

❧ What Went Down? ❧

Up in da South Side of Chi-town durin' da 1950s, a black family called da Youngers crammed into a stuffy two-bedroom apartment. And it sho ain't no small family. They got Walter and Ruth, who be married; their son, Travis; Walter's mama, Lena (or jus' "Mama," you know, since Walter's a mama's boy); and Walter's sista, Beneatha.

Erryone basically broke as a joke. Walter on da grind as a driver, but he barely make nuff money to support da family on they day-to-day shit. This apartment so damn crowded dat ain't **nobody** gettin' laid. No wonder errybody gettin' up in each otha's grills.

But thangs might be lookin' up for da Youngers. Mama got a **phat-ass** check comin' in da mail: ten Gs of insurance money, since her hubby up and died. Walter, tho, keep talkin' like it actually his; fool wanna use it to invest in a liqua store wit' one of his homies. His logic is simple: Errybody like gettin' fucked up, so investin' in a liquor store is a sho way to make it rain cash.

Ruth and Beneatha keep tellin' him to slow his roll, cuz dat money ain't his, but Walter too stubborn to listen. Plus, Mama ain't gonna be down wit' dat; she don't wanna throw dem stacks away on alcohol (da devil's bidness!). Naw, B, she wanna use the money to buy a house—cuz dat gonna make a **real** difference in her grandson Travis's life. Naw mean? And Mama wanna make sure Walter's sista got nuff of dat cash to go to medical school.

Walter ain't da only one feelin' like he gettin raw-dogged: Beneatha start gettin' crunk too, cuz Mama and Ruth keep baggin' on her. First, they bustin' her ass cuz she cain't keep her mind on one thang, and always jumpin' to somethin' new. Second, Mama and Ruth always talkin' up some clown name George Murchison, sayin' Beneatha betta holla back. But Bennie know this cat 'bout as cool as a bag of dicks. Beneatha piss Mama off **real good** by takin' da Lord's name in vain, and gets five across da face for it. Afta she leave, Ruth pass da fuck out! Turn out she pregnant, but keepin' it on da DL cuz da family ain't got no ends, and she don't know if they can keep da lil G.

Afta dat, some schola'ly hood name Joseph Asagai come over to chop game at Beneatha. He ain't so smooth, tho, cuz he spend most of da time givin' Bennie shit for sellin' out to white culture. But they still tight, and Asagai not only give her a Nigerian dress, but he also call her by a different name: Alaiyo.

Not much lata, what errybody waitin' for finally happen: dem fat stacks arrive. But shit get real when Walter come home and start ridin' his mama's ass beggin' her to use dat money for his liqua store. Mama call him out in front of errybody, wonderin' when black folk started thinkin' life mo' 'bout money than freedom. Then Mama get **real** crunk when she tell Walter 'bout Ruth's baby: 'parently, Ruth thinkin' 'bout havin' an abortion. Since Walter don't say a damn thang in response, Mama lay it down raw, callin' him a disgrace to da family. Wally jus' picks up his shit and walks out.

Eventually, dat rich playboy, George Murchison, come to scoop up Beneatha for some winin' and dinin'. Thang is, Bennie all dressed up in some fine Nigerian swag from Asagai. When George see Bennie sportin' those loose African threadz and the nappy fro she got under her headdress, he like, "Nuh-uh, bitch. Go change." While she gone, Walter, who been sippin' on dat crunk joose, start tryn'a talk big in fronta George, who jus' shake him off.

Then Mama bust in and say she put some money toward a swole new house in a fine neighborhood. All da family 'cept Walter get geeked, 'til they find out dat da new pad is in Clybourne Park—an all-white neighborhood.

Couple weeks lata, George back at da apartment and Beneatha start tryn'a get all philosophical on his ass. But George don't wanna hear none of dat; he jus' want a lil ooooo-wee. He tell her all dat book-talk is bullshit: jus' look good, get yo' degree, and das it. Now both Mama and Beneatha know dat even tho George swimmin' in Benjamins, fool shallow as they come.

Lata, da phone ring, and Ruth find out dat Walter ain't been to his job in three damn days. Instead, he jus' been wanderin' his sad-ass 'round da city. Mama start worryin' she doin' to Walter what erryone done to him his whole life: holdin' him back and not believin' in him. So to make him feel like he ain't such a fuck-up, Mama toss him summodat insurance money, sayin' she trust him to do da right thang.

As moving day get closer, erryone start feelin' pretty good. Ruth and Walter actually actin' like they can stand each otha for once. But all dat change when some honky named Karl Linder come a-knockin' and say da Youngers best not move to Clybourne Park. See, Lindner don't want no black folk jockin' da style of honest, hardworkin' whities. So Lindner try to bribe 'em wit' a stack of green, but da Youngers tell him to shove dat money right up his ass. They move whereva da hell they want.

Then one of Walter's homies name Bobo come to da apartment, and errybody find out some **real shitty** news: Walter spent all his daddy's money on dat liquor sto' even tho he said he wouldn't; not only dat, but Walter's bidness padna took all da money and got da hell outta town. Now there ain't no money for Beneatha's schoolin'.

Since errything gone to shit, Walter hit up Mr. Lindner again so he can take him up on his offer. But jus' when Walter 'bout to bend over for Lindner, Mama say dat if he gonna be a lil bitch, he gonna have to do it in front of his boy, Travis. Dat day, Walter's nuts grew three sizes; fool kick Lindner out once and for all, and get ready to move to Clybourne Park. Racist honkies be damned!

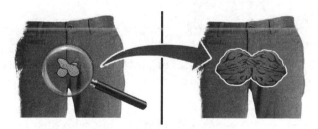

AND SO WALTER'S NUTS GREW THREE SIZES THAT DAY.

~ Themes 'n' Shit ~

DA POWER OF DREAMIN'

Some might say da main theme revolvin' 'round da question: "What gonna happen to somebody who got a dream dat neva happened?" Afta all, da play get its name from one of Langston Hughes poems, "Harlem," where he askin', What happens when yo dreams pass you by? Do yo dreams jus' shrivel up "like a raisin in a sun"? Do they "fester" and start smellin' like shit? Do they weigh down on a brutha's back till he collapse? Or do they "explode"?

Whether it cuz of society's racism and oppression, or some thug not bein' able to deal wit' da responsibilities dat come wit' raisin' a family, da prollem da same: How's a brutha gonna go on livin' afta his dream gone to shit?

To some, they life become jus' a stack of letdowns, and all dem dreams jus' dry up. As Mama and Ruth realizin', they ain't no realer truth than dreams not comin' true:

MAMA: "All the dreams I had 'bout buying that house and fixing it up. . . . None of it happen."
RUTH: "Yes, life can be a barrel of disappointments, sometimes."
(1.1.45)

Even Big Papa Walter, Mama's dead husband, who hustled 'round da clock, had to slow his roll—das why she describe him as a playa who could never catch up to dreams he had (46).

But for Walter, his dreams don't jus' dry up like a raisin in the sun, they "fester" in da sun and "stink" errything up. Walter got so much anger buildin' up inside dat he jus' 'bout to snap: "I want so many things that they are driving me kind of crazy. . . . The future stretched out in front of me. . . . full of *nothing*" (1.2.73–74).

When George say Walter wacked-out wit' bitterness, Walter get next-level pissed and break it down for him:

And you—ain't you bitter, man? Bitter? Man, I'm a volcano. Bitter? Here I am a giant—surrounded by ants! Ants who can't even understand what it is the giant is talking about.

(2.1.85)

WHAT REALLY FEED A BRUTHA AND KEEP 'EM GOIN'

One of this play's big ideas is dat without dreams, a playa ain't really a human bein'. Hansberry slingin' images of food to preach dat truth. See, food ain't all ya need to be healthy. Walter get all riled up when he's talkin' to Ruth 'bout dreams and life, and all she can say is, "Eat yo' eggs" (1.133–34).

There a special kinda nourishment dat only our dreams can give us. Ruth gotta realize dat even tho she a good wife, there are some thangs Walter need dat she jus' can't provide (2.1.88).

Beneatha also reppin' this idea dat dreams provide da nutrition dat food cain't. Asagai give her da African name Alaiyo, which mean One for Whom Bread [food] Is Not Enough (1.1.65).

DREAMS

PACKED FULL OF NUTRITION!

RACISM AND OPPRESSION

For da Younger family, chasin' they dreams and findin' themselves is a struggle cuz of all da racism and oppression 'round 'em. Walter feelin' his most down-and-out when he compare himself to white folk. It kill him dat all he can give Travis is "stories about how rich white people live" (1.1.340).

Ain't nobody representin' racism mo' dan dat backward-ass honky Karl Lindner, da tool from Clybourne Park. Even tho da Youngers good, hardworkin' peeps who got jus' as much a right to live in Clybourne Park as anybody else, Lindner treat 'em like they ain't shit (2.3.119).

Walter lata step up to Lindner and take back dat pride his mom and pops hustled so hard to build. Altho da Youngers won da battle 'gainst dem hat- erz, da war ain't even close to over. Yuh, da Youngers movin' on up to Clybourne Park, but they still gonna have to keep fightin' da hate. Linder say to dem, "I sure hope you people know what you're getting into" (3.1.149).

HATERZ GONNA HATE

"EXPRESS YO'SELF!"

Aside from all da otha bullshit da Youngers gotta beast through, da Younger family also gotta figger out who they be and how to define wut it mean to be black, po', proud, a respectful member of a family, a man, a woman, even a human.

Beneatha gotta go toe-to-toe wit' nearly all deez thangs. Da bitch of it is: It ain't jus' da man holding her down. Sometimes even her family don't understand her. Girl get laughed at by Ruth and Mama when she say she wanna find ways to express herself (1.1.48).

She even get called out from dat mothaland brutha Asagai: " 'I thought you were the most serious little thing I had ever seen. . . . 'Mr. Asagai, I am looking for my *identity*!' (*He laughs*)" (1.2.61–62).

Even tho he don't know it, Walter also tryn'a figger out who he really be. When fool po' up sum drank and hear some Nigerian jamz, he gets all turnt up: "I'm digging them drums . . . them drums move me! . . . In my *heart of hearts*—(*He thumps his chest*)—I am much warrior!" (2.178)

By da end, Walter finally figgered out who he is and who he wanna become. Like Mama say, "He finally come into his manhood today, didn't he? Kind of like a rainbow after the rain . . ." (3.1.151).

✍ Images 'n' Symbols ✍

DA YOUNGER CRIB

The Younger pad representin' how da family once was and how they like now. Da apartment, like errybody livin' in it, started off wit' care, love an' pride. As time go on, tho, all dem feelings get worn down by da world's bullshit and da oppression they suffa' through (1.1.23).

In da final scene, all da Youngers' junk packed away in boxes. Jus' as Walter stand on da line between pride and shame, love and cynicism, dem boxes also in a state of transition: literally movin' from one place to anotha. Will they stuff stay in da same tired place it been for years? It's all up to 'em. 'Specially Walter.

BENEATHA'S HAIR

In order to define who she is and throwback some of her African heritage, Beneatha cut off all her hair. Da way it was before was indicatin' dat she was becomin' part of da culture of da oppressor instead of buckin' it like she should. Asagai say of her hair, "You wear it well . . . very well . . . mutilated hair and all. . . . Were you born with it like that?" (1.2.61–62)

MAMA'S PLANT

Mama got a plant dat not only symbolizin' Walter and Beneatha but also expressin' how Mama be. It's tired, ain't got da nourishment it need cuz it's jus' trapped, but it keep on truckin' anyway.

Afta Walter and Bennie yellin' at each otha and slammin doors:

MAMA: My children and they tempers. Lord, if this little old plant don't get more sun than it's been getting it ain't never going to see spring again.

(1.1.40)

MAMA: Bennie and Walter. Like this little old plant that ain't never had enough sunshine or nothing . . .

(1.1.52)

Afta Ruth get word dat Mama jus' put some money down on a house, Mama get all geeked, sayin' dat da plant actually expresses **her**:

BENEATHA: That raggedy-looking old thing?
MAMA: It expresses ME!

(2.3)

✑ Shout-Outs! ✑

Givin' props to otha works dat preachin' da same truths as *A Raisin in the Sun*.

Classics

And so even though we face the difficulties of today and to-morrow, I still have a dream. It is a dream deeply rooted in the American dream.

I have a dream that one day this nation will rise up and live out the true meaning of its creed: "We hold these truths to be self-evident, that all men are created equal."

> —Docta Martin Luther King Jr.

Come on, America, ain't no barriers
Free the strings, let's see how freedom rings.

> —P. Diddy, "The American Dream"

REMIX

All da Younger crew gotta deal wit' unequal treatment from all da haterz around 'em. Whenever Walter cruisin' 'round town, he always peepin' white people his age dat don't seem no different from him. Da big difference, tho, is they got a phat bankroll and can do whateva da hell they want. Likewise Beneatha goin' all-out tryn'a make sure society don't forget dat da saying, "All men are created equal," **don't jus' apply to dudes**. Tryn'a realize dem dreams is what keep deez kids goin'; it's as necessary as air to breathe and food to eat.

✦ ✦ ✦

Classic

Insist on yourself; never imitate. Your own gift you can offer with the cumulative force of a whole life's cultivation, but of the adopted talent of another, you have only an extemporaneous, half possession.

—Ralph Waldo Emerson

REMIX

Asagai don't jus' hit up da Younger crib to lay da mack down on Beneatha. He also choppin' da same flows Emerson was, tellin' Beneatha dat she gotta drop all dat assimilationist jive and rep who she **really be.**

Hamlet

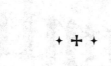

∽ So What's the Deal? ∽

Since he one of da **baddest** authors of all time, we gotta give Ol' Willy Shakes a lil extra love. Even tho mah boy's works **still** get mad props on da reg—and for good reason—ain't too many of 'em as popular as *Hamlet*. This shit's got it all: murder, deceit, comedy, and some heavy-hittin' themes, like life, death, and havin' da nuts to make da roughest decisions. Plus, it feature one of da most famous soliloquies of all time: Hammy's "to be, or not to be" speech.

Hamlet has got his hand **all up** in dat pop culture pie: in movies like *The Lion King* and *Star Wars*; TV shows like *Sons of Anarchy*; video games like Mass Effect and Borderlands; and in da works of literary big dawgs like Vonnegut, Joyce, Dickens, and David Foster Wallace.

Also, playin' Hamlet onstage is one of da best ways an actor can get street-certified **legit**. Summa da most throwed film actors of all time have put their cinema grind to da side to take on one a da realest challenges in da acting game. I'm talkin homeboys like Jude Law, Peter O'Toole, Richard Burton, Ralph Fiennes, Christopher Walken, Jon Voight . . . I could go on, playa.

❧ Homies ❧

HAMLET

Next in line to rock da crown of Denmark, and nephew of dat mothafucka Claudius, da new king. Hamlet pissed as hell dat his mama jumpin' inta bed wit' her dead hubby's bro and is ready to keep it street to avenge his pop's death. Thang is, Hamlet too busy delayin' and askin' himself all kindsa questions: Should he kill his own uncle? Should he forgive him? Fool got no idea 'bout what he should do. Matter of fact, Hamlet ain't never certain 'bout nothin'.

GHOST OF OL' KING HAMLET

This pasty-ass ghost cruisin' 'round da castle, hollerin' at da guard, and eventually bendin' Hamlet's ear. He tell Hamlet he gotta avenge his death by killin' his own uncle, Claudius. Only prollem is, Hamlet don't know if this thing's really da ghost of his daddy or jus' a demon messin' wit' his head.

CLAUDIUS

Old King Hamlet's brutha from da same motha. One night, Claudius po'ed up some poison joose in da king's ear. Now dat da king dead, Claudius nab da throne **and** Old Hamlet's wife, Gertrude.

GERTRUDE

Hamlet's mama, who knockin' boots wit' da man who iced her husband. Damn, girl.

HORATIO

Hamlet's homeboy, who he used to kick it wit' back in school. Hamlet always hittin' up this fool to tell him all kinda top secret shit. And this true-blue playa always keepin' it on da DL, cuz on da real, he jus' 'bout da only trustworthy person in this whole damn play. Maybe dat's why he da only big dawg dat survive at da end.

POLONIUS

Pops of Laertes and Ophelia. Also, da king's chamberlain—which basically mean he's da king's lapdog. Fool prolly know Claudius did some dirty shit to get da crown, but he don't care. He jus' loyal to whoever in power. What a bitch.

LAERTES

Polonius's son. This G don't fuck aroun' like Hamlet. When shit go south, he get straight down to bidness.

OPHELIA

Polonius's daughter. Her and Ham-ham use' to have a lil sweet thang, and a lotta folks think dat's why he actin' so cray. Eventually, Ophelia drowns: but ain't nobody know if she did da deed herself or accidentally fell into a buncha water.

FORTINBRAS

Da prince of Norway, who got beef wit' da old King Hamlet. Wit' a big-ass army at his back, he gonna take what's his. Homeboy gets it too, and end da play rockin' dat iced-out crown afta errybody dead.

ROSENCRANTZ AND GUILDENSTERN

Two of Hamlet's old-school homies. They pretend to be cool wit' Hamlet, but on da real, they jus' a buncha fakers workin' for Claudius.

Hamlet ain't stupid, tho. He get da jump on deez haterz and tricks 'em inta an early grave.

❦ What Went Down? ❦

Up at da castle in Elsinore, two guards name Bernardo and Marcellus been runnin' inta some weird-ass shit. So they holla' at they boy Horatio and say, "Mayne, you best get yo' ass out here. We peeped a **goddamn ghost** rollin' 'round like he own da place. And for real, it kinda look like ol' King Hamlet. Didnt' dat fool **jus'** die?"

Horatio like, "Da hell yo' stupid-asses been smokin'?" When da ghosts pops out again, erryone like, "**Oh shit, son!**" Horatio try to holla at it, but da ghost keeps its mouth **shut**. Horatio say, "Aight. Well. Since I ain't legit enough for this ghost to be talkin to, I guess we gotta get King Hamlet's son, Hamlet, out here.

Back in da castle, da ol' King Hamlet's brutha, Claudius, givin' a speech announcin' he da king now, since he jus' married da king's old biddy, Gertrude. Old Man Hamlet ain't even settled in his grave and Gertrude already shackin' up wit' da king's **brutha**. But dat royal oo-wee ain't da only thang on da new king's mind. Word on da street is da new boss of Norway, Fortinbras, gettin' prepped to wreck dem suckas in Denmark and take Claudius's newly snatched crown.

All by his lonesome, Hamlet start whinin' 'bout existence when some of his boys roll in and say, "Yo, Hammy, you gotta check this ghost. He look jus' like your old man."

And sho nuff, Hamlet's ghost-daddy show up and break it down

Gertrude GERTRUDE IS NOW SINGLE.
<u>9 minutes ago</u> · Comment · <u>Like</u> 12:01am

 **Gertrude is in a relationship with Claudius.**
12:02am

> **Hamlet** DA HELL?
> 11 minutes ago · Delete

for him raw: "Look. Some shit went down. My brutha, Claudius, stuck it to me by po'in' poison in my ear and now he's stickin' it in my woman—yo' mama. Only one thang to do, son. You gotta strap up and put a **toe tag** on dat fool Claudius." Jus' one catch, tho: Hamlet don't know if he can trust a damn word dat ghost sayin'.

Lata, Ophelia tell Polonius dat Hamlet been actin' whack. But Polonius jus' shrug it off and tell Ophelia dat it ain't no thang: Hammy's jus' jonesin' for summodat sweet nasty. Claudius decide to bring Hamlet's old-school homies Rosencrantz and Guildenstern to town so they can find out what's goin on inside Hamlet's dome.

When Hamlet runs inta deez fools, he ask, "Da hell y'all doin' here?" Dem fools say they there to see him, but Hamlet like, "Stop frontin'. You only here cuz my uncle shipped yo' asses ova here to snitch on me."

Word come dat some playas (literally, dawg—a troupe of actors) dun come to town. Afta some cogitatin', Hammy decide he can use dat crew to fine out if Claudius really iced his old man: In front of errybody, dem actors gonna put on a play called *The Murder of Gonzago,* where somebody po'in' poison joose up in Gonazago's ear to get down and dirty wit' Gonzago's lady—jus' like Claudius s'posedly did wit' Hamlet's pops and mama.

When Claudius watches dat murder play out, he busts ass outta da room real quick. Now Hamlet know dat Ghost-Daddy been spittin' da truth.

The Murder of GONZAGO
coughKingHamlet

All alone now, Claudius feelin' like a real bitch for killin' his bro, and starts prayin' to da man upstairs. Hamlet swangs on by, sees Claudius all by his lonesome, and start thinkin', "Now's my chance to **end** this sucka." But then he like, "Hold up. If I kill him while he prayin', he'll go to heaven, and heaven is **waaayy** too good for this fool."

Up in Gertrude's room, Polonius hide behind a curtain so he can listen to Hamlet and Gertrude conversatin'. Hamlet walk in, get all up in his mama's grill, and call her out for gettin' freaky wit' Claudius. Hammy get so crunk dat Polonius screams like a bitch. Thinkin' it's Claudius behind da curtain, Hamlet plunges dat sword right through da curtain, accidentally shankin' Polonius. Oops.

Then, Hammy see his daddy's ghost pop up, but since Gertrude cain't see it, she thinkin' Hamlet's lost his goddamn mind.

Claudius hears 'bout Hammy stabbin' Polonius and realize dat he prolly next. To get Hamlet da hell outta there, Claudius want Rosencrantz and Guildenstern not only to take Hamlet outta da kingdom, but also to **actually** take him out. Pop, pop, naw I'm sayin?

When Laertes hear 'bout his papa's death, he ready to kick ass and take names. He don't know who did da deed, but he don't give a

fuck, even if it da king himself—Laertes gonna git dat sucka. When he meet up wit' Claudius, da king whips out dat class-A bullshit and tell Laertes it was Hamlet who did his papa dirty.

Lata, Horatio get a letter from Hammy sayin' da ship to England got ganked by a buncha pirates, Rosencrantz and Guildenstern were some lil snitch-bitches who got what they deserved, and now he cruisin' back to Elsinore.

When Laertes discover Hamlet back in town, he get all geeked up to take dat sucka **out**. Claudius down for an old-school brawlin', so he set up a duel between da two of 'em.

And to make sure dat Hamlet stay down for da count, Claudius not only gonna soak Laertes's sword in poison, but he po' dat haterade into Hamlet's wine too. Jus' then, Gertrude bust in sayin', **"Ophelia dun drowned!"** Laertes like, **"For real? Sheeeiit."**

Durin' Ophelia's funeral, Laertes starts losin' his shit cuz they ain't give her a proper Christian burial. Word is she killed herself, so she cain't be buried like a good Christian. When Hamlet see who lyin' in dat coffin, he flip out, sayin' he loved Ophelia wit' all his heart. But on da real, he prolly jus' pissed he didn't hit it.

Lata, Hamlet tell Horatio how he escaped from his death sentence: He swapped da papers orderin' his own death wit' papers orderin' dat Rosencrantz and Guildenstern's die. So dem homies is dead now. Hamlet's stackin' those bodies like it's his job.

And here come anotha chance to add some to da pile: Hamlet and Laertes get to duelin', and Gertrude get so amped dat she takes a pull of dat poison syrup and dies. Laertes shanks Hamlet wit' his crunked-up blade, then Hamlet takes dat same blade and shanks him back. Now they both as good as dead. Right before Laertes take dat long dirt nap, he start snitchin' to Hammy sayin' all da poison was Claudius's doin'. So Hamlet stab Claudius wit' da sword, open his mouth, and make him down da rest of dat poison. Horatio peep all deez folk dyin', and decide he gonna jump in on da party; but Hamlet tell dat fool to chill: He gotta stay alive to tell errybody what happen.

Then Fortinbras of Norway roll inta da room, see practically errybody lyin' in chalk, and like, "Dafuq goin on in here? Nevermind. King me, bitches."

❧ Themes 'n' Shit ❧

LAERTES AND HAMLET: FOILS AND DADDY ISSUES

Aight: so on one hand we got Hamlet—fool s'posed to step up to da chump who killed his daddy and lay down dat street justice. But he never get off his ass and actually get shit done: he jus' walks his sad-ass around, all indecisive and shit.

Dat boy Laertes, tho . . . he don't fuck around. As soon as he find out his daddy, Polonius, got capped, he barrels onta Claudius's turf ready to bring da pain to **anyone**.

LAERTES: To hell, allegiance! Vows to the blackest devil!
. . .

Let come what comes. Only I'll be revenged.

(4.5.127, 131)

✦ SPARKY'S CLASSROOM ✦

What is a foil? There all kindsa ways to describe thangs, and one of da easiest for us to understan' somethin' is when there's some kinda comparison bein' made. A foil is when you got a character contrastin' wit' anotha so you can see betta what a playa's like.

Not only dat, but a "foil" is a kind of sword dat homies use in fencin', and when they pickin' swords for da duel, Hamlet even say:

I'll be your foil, Laertes. In mine ignorance
Your skill shall, like a star i'th' darkest night,
Stick fiery off indeed.

(5.2.192–194)

BEIN' ON LOCKDOWN

Laertes tell Ophelia she best not get too close to Hamlet, cuz even tho he royalty, he don't get to call all da shots. See, Hamlet don't even get to decide who he end up wit', cuz he might have to marry somebody for da good of da kingdom (1.3.14–24).

Since Hamlet was born a prince, he don't always get to choose who he gonna become; and in a lotta ways, his life ain't nothin mo' than a prison.

On da real, it ain't jus' Denmark that holdin' our boy down, it's the world itself. Afta all, Hamlet didn' **choose** to be born a prince. And there ain't nothin' he can do to 'scape his identity.

> HAMLET: Denmark's a prison.
> ROSENCRANTZ: Then is the world one.
> H: A goodly one, in which there are many confines, wards, and dungeons, Denmark being one o'th' worst.
> R: We think not so, my lord.
> H: Why, then 'tis none to you, for there is nothing either good or bad but thinking makes it so. To me it is a prison.
>
> (2.2.239–245)

JUS' CUZ IT DANK DON'T MEAN IT DON'T STANK

Peeps always goin' on 'bout disease up in this play to say somethin' is corrupt and twisted. When Hamlet ask his mama to not bullshit 'bout da awful shit she done, he tell her dat flatterin' words are jus' gonna make for a pretty outside, but a "rank corruption" on da inside, "[infectin'] unseen" (3.4.135–140).

Even tho thangs might **look** legit on da outside, there a big difference between **bein'** and **seemin'**, playa. We got somethin' dat **seem** like it healthy, but on da real, it ain't nothin' but rotten and corrupt on da inside.

TOO MANY QUESTIONS = TIME TO SIT ON MY ASS

Now, when it come to gettin' down to bidness, Hamlet would rather bitch and moan than get off his ass and kill Claudius.

HAMLET: . . . Yet I,
A dull and muddy-mettled rascal, peak
Like John-a-dreams, unpregnant of my cause,
And can say nothing—no, not for a king
Upon whose property and most dear life
A damned defeat was made. Am I a coward?

(2.2.543–548)

When Hammy spot Claudius prayin', he finally get da perfect chance to whoop dat ass. Instead of actually doin' it tho, he decide to chill: If Claudius die afta hittin' up God, he'll go to heaven, which Hamlet thinks is too good for dat ho. A lot of schola'ly hoods think this jus' anotha example of Hamlet bein' an indecisive bitch (3.4.75–95).

WHAT YO EYES TELL YOU AIN'T NECESSARILY TRUE

Like I say before, there's a big-ass difference between how somethin' **seems** and how it actually **is.** When Gertrude ask Hamlet why he seem so upset, Hamlet break her off a lil somethin':

HAMLET: Seems, madam? Nay, it *is*. I know not "seems."
. . .
But I have that within which passeth show.

(1.2.76; 85)

Polonius talkin' dat same jive wit' Ophelia, tellin' his daughta to watch her ass, cuz what someone **say** ain't mean shit 'bout what's in their heart or what they actually gonna **do** (1.4.126–134).

Claudius get a lil of dat seemin'-and-bein' action while he choppin' game wit' Rosencrantz and Guildenstern. Whether Hamlet's madness is real or a front, he **seem** like a different person to erryone who know him:

CLAUDIUS: . . . Something have you heard
Of Hamlet's transformation—so I call it,
Since not th'exterior nor the inward man
Resembles that it was.

(2.2.4–7)

❧ Images 'n' Symbols ❧

EARS 'N' LISTENIN'

Sometimes, openin' yo' trap can lead to danger; so some hoods, like Polonius, think dat openin' up yo' ears and listenin' is where it at. He say, "Give every man thine ear but few thy voice" (1.3.68).

But on da real, Polonius don't know da hell he talkin' 'bout, cuz it's dem ears dat lead to a lot of deaths. When Ghost-Daddy shootin' da shit wit'

Hamlet, he basically sayin', "Best watch out, cuz soon as you **hear** da words comin' outta my pale ghost lips, yo' life gonna be put on a whole new path, son."

HAMLET: Speak, I am bound to hear.
GHOST: So art thou to revenge when thou shalt hear.

(1.5.7–8)

And when Hamlet gettin' real on his mama's ass (not like that—fool ain't King Claudius), we seein' how jus' **hearin'** words can be so damn painful it's like somebody stuck you in da ears with a goddamn shiv (3.4.84–86).

All this ear shit get straight literal when we lookin' at how Claudius kill King Hamlet: by po'in' out some poison in his **ear**. Dat ain't da only poison dat Claudius slippin' in people's ears tho. Claudius be poisonin' Laertes by whisperin' some scandalous shit in his ears: Since King Claudius too much of a pussy to take down Hamlet himself, he use words to make Laertes do his dirty work for him (4.7.1–4).

At da end, da play do one of dem meta–mind fucks. It all finish wit' Hammy tellin' Horatio he gotta spread da word of what went down. So when Fortinbras drop in, Horatio like, "Say, bruh, open up yo' **ears** and lemme drop this story on you." So if Horatio actually tell Fortinbras what's up, he'd have to retell da whole damn play **all over again**.

HORATIO: And let me speak to th' yet unknowing world
How these things came about.

(5.2.323–324)

⸺ Say What? ⸺

Classic

Afta Gertrude and Claudius tryn'a cheer up Hammy:

> HAMLET: . . . O God, O God,
> How weary, stale, flat, and unprofitable
> Seem to me all the uses of this world!
> Fie on't, ah fie, fie! 'Tis an unweeded garden
> That grows to seed.
>
> (1.2.132–136)

REMIX

> HAMLET: Goddaym. What a shit world.

✦ ✦ ✦

Classic

One of da most famous quotes you ever gonna hear or read:

> HAMLET: To be, or not to be; that is the question:
> Whether 'tis nobler in the mind to suffer
> The slings and arrows of outrageous fortune,
> Or to take arms against a sea of troubles,
> And, by opposing, end them. To die, to sleep—
> No more, and by a sleep to say we end
> The heartache and the thousand natural shocks
> That flesh is heir to—'tis a consummation
> Devoutly to be wished.
>
> (3.1.58–66)

REMIX

HAMLET: Should I live or die? Am I a balla who gonna keep fightin', no matter how raw shit get, or should I jus' say "fuck it," and peace outta this world? Yeah. Prolly dat one.

✦ ✦ ✦

Classic

When Claudius tryn'a pray for forgiveness, and Hamlet watchin' like a creeper:

My words fly up, my thoughts remain below.
Words without thoughts never to heaven go.

(3.3.97–98)

REMIX

CLAUDIUS: Shit don't matter if you don't mean it.

✦ ✦ ✦

Classic

When Gertrude doin' a real shitty job tryn'a cheer up her son:

QUEEN GERTRUDE: Good Hamlet, cast thy nightly color off,
And let thine eye look like a friend on Denmark.
Do not for ever with thy vailèd lids
Seek for thy noble father in the dust.
Thou know'st 'tis common—all that lives must die,
Passing through nature to eternity.

(1.2.68–73)

REMIX

Time destroy errrything. If it lives, it gonna die. Dat's jus' da way it go. Ashes to ashes, dust to dust, mayne. Nothin' last forever.

✦ ✦ ✦

Classic

When Hamlet cruisin' through a graveyard and find da skull of one of his boys:

> HAMLET: Alas, poor Yorick. I knew him, Horatio—a fellow of infinite jest, of most excellent fancy. He hath borne me on his back a thousand times; and now, how abhorred my imagination is! My gorge rises at it. Here hung those lips that I have kissed I know not how oft. Where be your gibes now, your gambols, your songs, your flashes of merriment that were wont to set the table on a roar? Not one now to mock your own grinning?
>
> (5.1.171–177)

REMIX

Damn, B. Where yo dead-ass at now?

✦ ✦ ✦

Classic

When Polonius tryn'a make sure dat some hood keep an eye on his son:

> POLONIUS: . . . See you now,
> Your bait of falsehood takes this carp of truth;

And thus do we of wisdom and of reach
With windlasses and with assays of bias
By indirections find directions out.
So, by my former lecture and advice,
Shall you my son.

(2.1.61–67)

REMIX

Want da truth? You gotta lie yo' ass off for it.

✦ ✦ ✦

Fahrenheit
451

＋ ✦ ✦

⤳ So What's the Deal? ⤳

Now, while a lotta dystopian books gonna make you stain yo' draws 'bout da future, Ray Bradbury's *Fahrenheit 451* do it a lil differently. See, da government didn't jus' go and seize control all dick-tater like and turn us into drones. Naw, blood. Errybody in da world jus' handed over they freedom, hopin' for an easier, quieter life.

Folks usually jivin' dat this book all 'bout censorship and book burnin', but they missin' da big picture. Brady-B's novel is mo' 'bout what happens when peeps try to pursue a life where there's jus' **one** answer to a question; where errything painless and easy; where da combination of mass media and tryn'a keep folks from gettin' butthurt mean dat you can't say or do a damn thang; and 'bout how all of this mess lead to a darker, emptier life than you eva seen.

❧ Homies ❧

GUY MONTAG

Da hero of da book. At first, Montag jus' anotha drone who doin' what da man tellin' him. But afta meetin' Clarisse McClellan, Montag start questionin' life and why he so damn unhappy. All this soul-searchin' send Montag down a head-trip full of books and blazin', which make him reject all da comforts he use to have and rebel against a society he cain't escape.

CLARISSE McCLELLAN

Montag's seventeen-year-old neighbor who aint' like any otha gal he met before. She question da idea of happiness dat Montag been fed all his life, and force Montag to look at da world wit' a new pair of eyes. Not long afta Montag start actin' out, Clarisse disappear for good. Ain't nobody know what happen to her.

CAPTAIN BEATTY

Montag's boss man at da fire department. This fool seen it all: includin' lotsa cats questionin' authority and readin' books—so Montag ain't da first thug Beatty's had to tussle wit'.

Captain Beatty don't jus' bend over wit' a smile for da man, tho. What make this sucka so dangerous is dat he can see right through this crooked-ass society he upholdin', and what make him so sad is dat he goin' through da motions anyway.

MILDRED MONTAG

Montag's dull-as-shit-wife. Ain't no betta example of da type of person dat this society pump out: all Mildred do is watch TV and pop pillz 24/7. She get upset when people throw out new ideas, and she don't even stand by her man when he tryn'a buck da system. Matter of fact, bitch even rat him out.

PROFESSOR FABER

An old teach dat Montag had a run-in wit' back in da day. Now dat Montag join da righteous book-lovin' cause, he hit up Faber, they get tight, and Faber put him on da path to a brighta future.

∽ What Went Down? ∽

Model Citizen

"It was a pleasure to burn" (3)—afta readin' da book's first line, you might be thinkin': "Please tell me this Bradbury fool goin' on 'bout lightin' up a J" . . . Sadly, dat ain't what this book 'bout. Four-fitty-one take place in a futuristic America where our main man, Guy Montag, hustlin' as a fireman. 'Cept in this society, firemen don't put out no fires. 'Stead, they all strapped wit' fire-spittin' hoses dat burn shit down—'specially books. See, up in this crazy hood, readin' books is illegal, but doin' brainless shit is encouraged. Da man gonna tell you and erry-body else to jus' chill out, turn yo' brain off, and think what da TV tell you to think.

One day, Montag walkin' home from his daily grind when he meet a seventeen-year-old girl named Clarisse McClellan. 'Stead of jus' spittin' some bullshit she heard on television like most people do, Clarisse actually question da way thangs be and talk all kinda smack 'bout da establishment. She make Montag realize dat he never use his brain, and he actually unhappy as hell.

Montag's mind be fourteen kindsa fucked afta dat convo wit' Clarisse. And fuel jus' get added to da fire when Montag get home: Brutha peep his wife, Mildred, passed da hell out afta poppin' too many pillz. Montag gotta call some homies wit' machines to pump Mildred's stomach and put her back on her feet.

Next day, Mildred so jacked up and unhappy dat she don't even remember tryn'a kill herself. When Montag try to talk to her 'bout what went down, she basically jus' crank da TV volume and get back to bidness.

Ain't no thang to Montag tho, since he chillin' wit' Clarisse on da reg now. All da while, Montag's eyes gettin' opened up to da world and people 'round him. Errything all gravy until five, six, then seven days go by wit'out word from Clarisse. Da hell?

Lata, Montag and his firemen posse get a call dat some hag been hoardin' books up in her crib. So they gear up and cruise over to da spot, ready to blaze. Captain Beatty's crew, which include Montag, soak all her papers in kerosene. They 'bout to take her away and burn her shit to da ground, but she like, "Nuh-uh, playa. Dat ain't how this is goin' down." Then, bitch whips out a match and light herself and all her shit on fire! **Damn, girl—get it.** Before errything went up in flames, Montag snagged a lil readin' material on da sly.

Now Montag **really** confused. Not only is he wonderin' why someone would wanna die over a bunch of books, but he also askin' himself, "Am I outta my damn mind? What am I doin' stealin' books?" Somehow, shit get even worse for our boy: Montag feelin' mo' and mo' dead inside, 'specially when he at home. He try to make errything a lil betta by havin' some sweet talk wit' his biddy, Mildred. Prollem is they like strangers to each otha now, even tho they been livin' togetha for years. Then Montag find out dat Clarisse prolly dead, and her family gone.

Since Montag **definitely** feelin' like a big bag of shit, he decide he gonna play hooky dat day . . . dat is, until Montag's boss, Beatty, show up at his front door and start mad-doggin' him. Afta he give Montag a lil history lesson 'bout how da world fell apart, he basically say, "Look, Montag, I know you packin' books up in this joint. All good, playa, errybody been there before. You got twenty-four hours to toss dat shit, and we straight."

Afta dat, Montag come clean to his woman. He say, "Millie. Check it. It ain't jus' **one** book I been hidin'. I got a whole bunch. Why don't you peep game at deez, and see what you think?" They look through 'em, and Montag decide to ring up some playa he ran into back when: an old English teach name Faber. They chat for a while, and Faber give Montag a lil earpiece dat gonna let 'em communicate 24/7.

When Montag get back to his spot, Mildred chillin' wit' two friends. Since Guy finally seein' da light, he wanna share da knowledge; so he shut off da TV, try to get errybody to actually talk to each otha, and then read 'em some poetry. Mildred get crunk on Montag's ass, cuz one of her friends starts weepin' while Guy is readin', and erryone has to go home.

Next time dat Montag go to work, he decide he gonna try to trick Beatty: He hand over jus' **one** of da books from his pad, not all of 'em, thinkin' errything all good now since Beatty don't know no betta.

But Beatty ain't yo' average sheep—he a wolf. Beatty tell Montag to come along for a special fireman ride, and end up wipin' dat smirk right offa Montag's face: they park dat hoopty in fronta **Montag's house**. Mildred sold his ass **out**.

Beatty all like: "You had yo' chance, son. I'm gonna watch you burn this dump down, then I'm gonna arrest yo' ass." But Montag's had it. Fool lights up his hose, point it toward Beatty, and turns dat punk into a pile of dirt.

Montag try to flee da scene, but not before da "hound"— some mechanical dog-cop thang— shank him in da leg. Montag bust

𝕿𝖍𝖚𝖌 𝕷𝖎𝖋𝖊

out his flame Glock again, makes robo-dog his bitch, and barely get his ass outta there.

Not knowing what he gonna do, Montag run over to Faber's place and Faber like, "Look, bruh, you best swim yo' white ass down da river and join up wit' some book-lovin' hobos." Yeah. For real.

Montag do jus' dat, and become a book-memorizin' gangbanga. See, all deez bruthas believe dat human bein's got photographic memories—you jus' gotta clear all da unnecessary shit outta yo' dome to use it. This posse, led by a dude name Granger, all packin' away mad book knowledge so they can help rebuild da world one day.

Turns out dat day ain't so far off. Da city dat Montag jus' bailed from gets a ton of bombs dropped on it, puttin' erryone in da dirt. At da end, Montag and his new bloods start makin' they way back to dat heap to start rebuildin'.

✎ Themes 'n' Shit ✎

TWO SIDES TO ERRY COIN

When Beatty drop in on Montag's crib, he school him good on how shit went sideways in da old world and why thangs are da way they are now (60–61). See, when peeps had to think 'bout there bein' mo' than one answer to a question, they got confused as fuck. And wit' confusion came unhappiness. So da world Montag and Beatty livin' in now give you **jus' one** solution to erry problem. Much easier that way, naw mean?

As Montag start becoming mo' conscious of da world round him, he start seein' dat backin' jus' one solution to erry problem is too damn simple—there be **two sides to errything**, even himself.

He felt his body divide itself into a hotness and a coldness, a softness and a hardness, a trembling and a not trembling, the two halves grinding one upon the other. (24)

This *duality* jam ain't jus' seen in people, but in shit like silence and fire too.

✦ SPARKY'S CLASSROOM ✦

When you lookin' at two thangs opposed to each otha or contrastin', you peepin' duality, son: like light and darkness, hot and cold, silence and loud-ass shit. All kinda art—not jus' literature—got duality.

In some instances, silence standin' in to show dat somethin' got no life and no emotion, like Montag point out when he get back home to Mildred. His whole crib is a tomb "where no sound . . . could penetrate" (11).

But righ' hurr, when Montag start chillin' wit' da book-lovin' hobo crew, silence somethin' good (146). Errybody silent, but not in dat cold, dead way. Naw, son. This is da kind of silence dat happen when people shut da fuck up and carefully consider somethin'. So this silence ain't got nothin to do wit' death, padna. It's all 'bout life, sincerity, thoughtfulness, and creativity.

ONE BIG-ASS CULTURE

When Beatty mean-muggin' Montag up in his crib, he droppin' some raw truth 'bout why da world is da way it is. Once information spread to erryone through radio, TV, Internet, and otha shit like dat, thangs started going whack.

Cuz soon as peeps get a lil taste of dat fast 'n' easy information, they gotta consume **errything** they can get they hands on. And since modern technology makin' it so dat **erryone** can experience it at da same time, people inevitably gonna start bitchin'. Da more peeps who see somethin', da more complaints you gonna hear (54).

Fahrenheit 451 – Thug Notes Summary and Analysis

▶ Subscribe

TOP COMMENTS (14)

BillyTheKid847 10 months ago
This video is the biggest piece of crap I've ever seen in my life. U suck.
Reply · 47 👍 👎

GrumpyDan32 8 days ago
How offensive and ridiculous. You should be ashamed.
Reply · 18 👍 👎

MarcieRoxy82 8 days ago
everything here is a pos, you should stop makin vids
Reply · 54 👍 👎

Da crooked-ass dystopia dat Montag find himself in wasn't created by an all-powerful government. Naw, this world was ushered in by all da sensitive bitches dat get butt-hurt over da stupidest shit: "There was no dictum, no declaration, no censorship, to start with, no! Technology, mass exploitation, and minority pressure carried the trick, thank God" (57–58, 59).

SLOWIN' YO' ROLL

Montag and homies livin' in a world where errybody gotta have they fix of stimulation **fast and on da reg**. Since peeps worldwide always focusin' on immediate gratification, they ain't even da time to put a goddamn thought togetha. Clarisse call Montag out for dat very thang (8–9).

Da batshit crazy speed dat da world movin' at don't jus' affect Montag's relations with othas, but erry damn part of his life (54–56).

KNOWIN' OTHAS

One of *Fahrenheit*'s main jams is dat ain't nobody know anybody else. Strangers don't talk to strangers, Montag barely even talk to his wife, and people don't even know themselves. Like Clarisse uncle say, people are jus' like tissues to errybody: "Blow your nose . . . wad them, flush them away, reach for another" (17).

Ain't no betta symbol for this idea than when Mildred tries to **off** herself by throwin' back a whole bottle of pillz. When the doctas swang by, they stick a buncha machines all up in her body. Penetratin' somebody you ain't know or care 'bout is as invasive as it gets.

While he watchin' deez randos go to town on his wife (14–15), Montag realize how jacked-up da world has become: "Nobody knows anyone. Strangers come and violate you" (16).

✒ Images 'n' Symbols ✒

FIRE

Fahrenheit 451 is so fulla flame dat even its title reppin' dat blaze: 451 degrees Fahrenheit is da temp at which paper burn.

451°
fahrenheit

Thang is, fire always changin' shape and got lotsa different uses. Likewise, fire as a symbol got lotsa different meanin's up in this text.

For big-dawg Beatty, fire is beautiful cuz it's mysterious, don't stop, and destroys erry damn thang in its path. Fire is pretty damn boss.

It's perpetual motion. . . . If you let it go on, it'd burn our lifetimes out. . . . It's a mystery. . . . Its real beauty is that it destroys responsibility and consequences. (115)

And at first, Montag thinkin' da same thang. Ain't nothin get him harder than strappin up wit' dat hose and blazin' shit to da ground (3).

As time go on, tho, Montag start seein' dat fire ain't jus' 'bout destruction; it can also give life and warmth (145).

Montag also seein' the legit side of fire when he lookin' at Clarisse's face and glowin' eyes. They got a "constant light. . . . not the hysterical light of electricity but . . . the strangely comfortable and rare and gently flattering light of the candle" (7).

HOW DA BOOK SPLIT UP
Part One: "The Hearth and the Salamander"

Hearths usually symbolizin' home: a place where you and yo' fam come togetha, stay warm, show each otha love, and keep dem swishers lit. But for Montag, da home definitely **not** where da heart (or hearth) is. Instead of his crib reppin' life, love, and comfort, home be a place of death and alienation. He call it "a mausoleum . . . [in] complete darkness, not a hint of the silver world outside, the windows tightly shut, the chamber a **tomb**-world" (11).

Part Two: "The Sieve and the Sand"

In part two, Montag have a non-drug-induced flashback to when he was a lil thug tryn'a fill a sieve wit' sand. No matter how hard the lil G tries, da sieve **jus' end up empty** (78).

Dat memory busts into Montag's dome when he tryn'a memorize da Bible.

> He remembered the terrible logic of that sieve. . . . If you read fast and read all, maybe some of the sand will stay in the sieve. (78)

This image ain't jus' 'bout stackin' knowledge; it also 'bout what you po' into relationships and what kinda love two peeps share. Part two open wit' Montag readin' wit' his biddy Mildred. Montag actually read out loud a passage 'bout this same thang:

> We cannot tell the precise moment when friendship is formed. As in filling a vessel drop by drop, there is at last a drop which makes it run over; so in a series of kindnesses there is at last one which makes the heart run over. (71)

This shit right hurr relevant in two ways:
1. It show how empty his relationship wit' his woman has become.
2. It fo'shadowing how fulfillin' his relationship wit' Faber gonna be lata in this section.

Part Three: "Burning Bright"
Since this a book all 'bout blazin', it's pretty damn obvious dat part three, "Burning Bright," talkin' 'bout fire. But that ain't all, son. It could also be a throwback to a poem by William Blake called "The Tyger," dat start, "Tyger! Tyger! burning bright / In the forests of the night."

One way to look at Willy B's Tyger is like a symbol for da human imagination: creative, destructive, and complex as hell. This fool so throwed dat no hand or eye can hold him down. And Montag da same way: ain't none of society's laws can hold this playboy down; naw, cuz. Fool burns too bright.

❧ Shout-Outs! ❧

Givin' props to otha works dat preachin' da same truths as *Fahrenheit 451*.

Classic

[T]he world "was ever, is now, and ever shall be, an ever-living
Fire." But fire is something continually changing, and its per-
manence is rather that of a process than that of a substance.
        —Bertrand Russell in his *History of Western Philosophy*,
    talkin' 'bout an old-school Greek philosopher name Heraclitus

REMIX

Bradbury musta' been **real down** wit' this kinda fire-talk: Beatty's
got a real hard-on for fire's neverendin' motion and da changes it
make to errything it touch; and like Clarisse show Montag, our lives
ain't meant to be static and tomb-like; we s'posed to dance and flicker.

✦ ✦ ✦

Classic

"There will be pain for us all; but it will not be all pain, nor
will this pain be the last. We and you too . . . will have to pass
through the bitter water before we reach the sweet. But we
must be brave of heart and unselfish, and do our duty, and all
will be well!"

                                            —Bram Stoker, *Dracula*

REMIX

If Montag wanna spend da rest of his life livin' in a gangsta's paradise, he gonna have to slay monsters inside and out: all da poisonous

thoughts he been pumped wit' by a jacked-up society, Mildred and Beatty's ignorance and cynicism, and even some sort of gnarly robo-pooch.

✦ ✦ ✦

Classic

OTHELLO: . . . Thou hast set me on the rack.
I swear 'tis better to be much abused
Than but to know't a little.

. . .

I saw't not, thought it not; it harmed not me.
I slept the next night well, fed well, was free and merry.
I found not Cassio's kisses on her lips.
He that is robbed, not wanting what is stol'n,
Let him not know't and he's not robbed at all.
                    —William Shakespeare, *Othello* (3.3.340–349)

REMIX

Is ignorance really bliss? Depend who you ask. Mildred is happy as can be chillin' in front of a buncha TV screens iced out on pillz 24/7; or at least, she think she is. Like Montag find out, ignorance jus' look like bliss on the outside; but underneath, peeps without any substance are jus' hollow inside.

✦ ✦ ✦

Classic

What's still more awful is that a man with the idea of Sodom in his soul does not renounce the ideal of the Madonna, and his heart may be on fire with that ideal, genuinely on fire, just as in his decays of youth and innocence. Yes, man is broad, too broad, indeed. I'd have him narrower.

—Fyodor Dostoevsky, *The Brothers Karamazov*

REMIX

Man is a walkin' contradiction, who got a never-endin' war ragin' inside him at all times. Montag knows he got warrin' elements inside him, and eventually he realize dat's **exactly** what make him a whole person.

The Catcher in the Rye

✦ ✠ ✦

❦ So What's the Deal? ❦

Soon as *Catcher* hit da streets, publishers were slangin this shit off da shelves like it was da dankest of da dank. Book was numba one on da *New York Times* bestseller list for thirty weeks **in a row**. If you sneak a peek at any literary big-dawg's list of top novels, you'll prolly see *Catcher* on it, and wit' good reason: J. D. Salinger's best work packed wit' legit truth 'bout loneliness, loss, and da lies of society.

Both *Time* magazine and da Modern Library say it got enough swagger to be one of da hundred best novels of da twentieth century. And da book **still** sell 'bout a quarter million copies each year.

But it ain't been all love for ol' Holden. Lotsa folks were, and still are, straight **buggin'** 'bout kids readin' this book. See, peeps got they shit in a bunch cuz Holden got such a filthy mouth and always sayin' "fuck you" to da establishment. All this bitchin' and moanin' mean dat lotsa schools ripped da book from reading lists. What a buncha phonies.

⤳ Homies ⤳

HOLDEN CAULFIELD

This sixteen-year-ol' thug is one of da loneliest cats in all of literature. He got his ass tossed outta school for not givin' a **fuck** and flunkin' almost errything. Holden usually bitchin' 'bout all da fakers and phonies puttin' up a front in this crooked-ass world. Even tho Holden ain't too fond of most peeps, dude really like kids; unlike adults, kids **always** keepin' it real. Apparently, Holden had some kinda breakdown, so he tellin' da story from a psychiatric ward or somethin'.

PHOEBE CAULFIELD

Holden's ten-year-old baby sista and one of da few peeps dat Holden think actually understand him. She always on his mind, and somehow always put a smile on Holden's lonely-ass face.

ALLIE CAULFIELD

Holden's younger brutha who died of leukemia a couple years back. Holden had mad love for this playa, and his death fucked Holden up real good. Losin' a brutha hard no matter how stone-cold you is.

ACKLEY

Holden's schoolmate who always showin' up to Holden's crib uninvited and jus' linger. He got a nasty, pimply face and like to go off 'bout God knows what. Holden try to get him to bounce, but this fool jus' cain't take a hint.

STRADLATER

Holden's blowhard roommate. Stradlater ain't so good at da school game, but he sho as hell good at da lady game. He ask Holden to write his English paper for him while he try to get fresh with a girl Holden used to holla at. Then he bitch cuz he don't like what Holden wrote. What a dick.

D. B. CAULFIELD

Holden's older bro who grindin' as a screenwriter up in Hollywood. He never actually show up in da book, but Holden always givin' him props and talkin' 'bout his fat stacks.

SALLY HAYES

A girl Holden know for a while who got a real nice boo-tay. Holden don't seem to think she very smart, but dat prolly cuz he wanna get freaky wit' her and she ain't putting out.

MR. SPENCER

One of Holden's teachers from prep school who try to tell him to get off his ass and actually start bustin' it.

MR. ANTOLINI

One of Holden's back-when teachers. Holden think he a real smart dude. He care a lot 'bout Holden and is down to chill and give him advice. Shit goes south, maybe in mo' way than one, when Holden wake up thinkin' dat Mr. Antolini coppin' a feel on him. They cool, but they ain't **that** cool.

❧ What Went Down? ❧

It all start up in psych ward or somethin', where our narrator, Holden Caulfield, tryn'a chill afta gettin' "pretty run-down." We don't know exactly what happened, but this playa snapped. Now he gonna tell us 'bout all da crazy shit dat jacked him up real good and got his ass locked up.

Back in high school, Holden went to some prissy, high-dolla' private place where he was flunkin' jus' 'bout erry one of his classes—'**cept English, yo!** To be straight up 'bout it, this fool jus' don't give a fuck.

Jus' as he chunkin' deuce to dat trap of a school, he hit up one of his teachers, Mr. Spencer, who invited him back to his spot. Spence start preachin' to Holden 'bout how he gotta get his shit together and start crackin' dem books so he don't turn out to be a bustah. He say, "Look, Holden, life is a game and if you wanna live large, you gonna have to play by da rules." Holden jus' shake off dat hata, since he know it ain't no game if you keep it hood.

So Holden head back to his dorm room, when some bruh named Ackley show his nasty pizza-face. This fool's grungy-ass always bargin' into Holden's room, gettin' all up in his bidness, and messing wit' Holden's shit.

Then Holden's roomie, Stradlater, walk in and say he gonna get a fine piece of ass tonight, so he gotta get pretty. Since this lazy-ass ain't got much time, he be all like, "Say, Holden, you wanna hook a brutha up and write my English paper for me? Da topic don't matter none."

Lata, Holden oblige Stradlater and start writin' his paper. Holden cain't think of nothin' to write 'bout, so he jus' describe a baseball mitt dat use' to belong to his lil brutha, Allie. Holden start reminiscin' 'bout dat fool, and we get the lowdown: A couple years back, Holden's bro Allie got hit wit' a nasty case of leukemia, and now he chillin' six feet deep. Holden still go on all da time 'bout how hard Allie use' to thug. In fact, Holden got so turnt up da night dat Allie died, he slept in da garage and smashed up all da windows wit' his bare hands.

When Stradlater roll back in afta tryn'a get some play, he take one look at dat paper and all like, "Yo, Caufield, dafuq is this shit? A baseball glove? Da hell, son?" Holden and Stradlater start ridin' each otha's nuts, and da next thang Holden know, he throwin' down wit' Stradlater. Afta Stradlater make Holden a bloodied-up lil bitch, Holden hit up Ackley before leavin' da school for good.

Holden get his ass outta there, but decide he don't wanna go back to his mom and pop's crib yet: so he set up shop in NYC at a hotel called da Edmont. Outta his window, Holden peepin' all kinda shit: a dude tryin' on women's clothes and anotha couple getting freaky by spittin' in each otha's faces. Whateva raises yo pillah, naw mean?

Anyway, Holden so riled up now dat he hit up some girl named Faith, cuz homies say she fuck anything dat moves. Too bad for Holden, dat jus' ain't da case. Holden get shut down, but go back on the prowl since he need to get dat nut **tonight**.

Still sportin' balls da size of watermelons, Holden decide he gonna go downstairs to scope out da lounge. While Holden gettin' ready, he start thinkin' 'bout dialin' his ten-year-ol' sista, Phoebe, since he figger dat she da only one he can talk sense wit'. But she prolly snoozin' hard-core, **and** he don't wanna take a chance of catchin' his parents.

Holden get downstairs and try to spit game at some fine biddies from outta town, but they ain't feelin' it and give our boy da cold shoulda. All he end up wit' is a bill for they dranks. Holden decide to swang over to da club where his bruh D.B. use' to chill. He take a taxi to get there, and ask da driver where da ducks in Central Park go when it get real cold. Holden don't get no answers, tho. When he get to da club, all he hear is people talkin' 'bout phony bullshit. Why people gotta be such fakers? So our boy get da hell out.

Back at da hotel, Holden takin' da elevator back up to his room when the operator like, "Psst. Say, bruh, whatchoo know 'bout dat oowee? For five dollas, I got a girl dat'll take **real** good care of you. Naw mean?" Holden be all like, "FIVE DOLLAS? Shiiit, that's a deal, man."

While most bruthas would be all geeked up waitin' for some poontang to knock on they door, Holden straight buggin' cuz he ain't busted his cherry yet. Afta a while, dat ho come a-knockin' on his door. Her name Sunny and she start getting butt-ass nekkid; but Holden jus' choke like a bitch and don't seal da deal. He try to slang dat five-spot her way and get her outta his room, but she want mo' money! When Holden all like, "Oh, hell naw!" Sunny leave all pissed. Holden jus' lay back and start lightin' up. A lil lata, Sunny bust back in wit' her pimp, Maurice, who smack Holden up, take dat cash, and bail. Dude **actually** got pimp-slapped!

Still backed up like a Catholic priest, Holden decide to hit up some gal he know named Sally Hayes, and they set up a time to hook up. In da meantime, Holden strollin' down da street and pick up an album for his lil sista, Phoebe. He see some lil kid jus' cruisin' along droppin' some sick beats. All a sudden, Holden start to feel a lil betta: it's nice to see a mini-thug jus' doin' his thang, ign'ant of da world's whack-ass ways.

Holden decide he wanna drop in on his sista, Phoebe, so he hit up da museum where she s'posed to be wit' her school. While he there, Holden peep some model Indians and Eskimos that he think are real tight.

Then Holden meet up wit' Sally and start headin' to da theater. On da way, Holden get a lil lip action. **Playa playa!** While they there, tho, Sally start flirtin' wit' some lame-ass chump from uptown. **Definitely** time to get da fuck outta there. But instead of kickin' Sally to da curb, Holden jus' brings da date to a different place. Even though Holden usually ain't down with dat kind of phony shit, he know dat ass is fine. And as all scholars agree, a fine ass go a long way.

LITERATURE QUARTERLY REVIEW

A fine ass go a long way.

But it ain't long til dealin' wit' all of Sally's and the world's fake-ass bullshit jus' too much for Holden. Outta nowhere, Holden goin' off 'bout how much he hate errything 'round him, and errybody in society jus' a bunch of phonies. Dude try to take his game next-level and say him and Sally should run away to a cabin together. When she tell him he actin' a straight fool, Holden start screamin' at her, and call her a royal pain in da ass (for real [133]). Holden feel a lil bad when she start cryin', but then he start laughin' for no reason! Sally get so pissed that she jus' peaces out. Damn, Holden—you supposed to hit it, **then** quit it . . . you forgot the best part, playa.

Holden keep wanderin' 'round, tryn'a connect wit' **somebody**, and decide to jus' head over to Central Park. He start marinatin' on da ducks, his bro Allie, and how jacked-up he and his mama got afta Allie's death.

Still wantin' to talk to Phoebe, Holden truck it back home to his folks' place. When he see Pheebs, she all amped dat Holden back from school. She start layin' all sorta talk on him 'bout what she been up to. And like he always do, Holden start talkin' 'bout how erry-body at school phony 'cept him. Phoebe like, "If you always hatin' on errything, what do you actually like?" Da only thang Holden can think of is Allie, and Phoebe call him out for not likin' anythin' on da earth—jus' peeps and thangs dat you cain't have. When Phoebe ask Holden what he wanna be, Holden start talkin' 'bout how he imagine himself in a field full of rye where he catchin' kids while they fallin' off a cliff. Deep.

Holden tell Phoebe dat he jus' gotta get his white ass outta New York, so he give her his red hunter's hat and bounce to his old teach Mr. Antolini's place.

At Antolini's crib, Holden start runnin' his mouth again 'bout all dem haterz at school and why he got kicked out. But Antolini like, "Look, bruh, you gotta get yo shit together—you headin' for a gnarly end, and I don't wanna see you go out like dat." They say good night. Holden fall asleep, but wake up in da middle of da night; when he do, Mr. Antolini feelin' up his head. Holden freaks da fuck out, start to feel even mo' depressed than he normally do, and jus' keep walkin' 'round da city.

Before he roll out to da West, Holden go to see Phoebe one last time. She all like, "Take me with you, bro." But he like, "Naw, cain't do, lil sis." Then she give back the huntin' hat and give Holden da cold shoulder. Dat shit jus' 'bout kills Holden, so he take her to a carousel they use' to visit wit' D.B. and Allie. Phoebe hop on, go round and round, and Holden feel jus' 'bout as happy as he ever has.

All of da sudden—**bam**. We back in da present day, wit' Holden chillin' wherever da hell he be, tryn'a get his mind straight. Holden say he could talk 'bout what da future hold, but he ain't gonna. . . . Talkin' 'bout dat shit jus' make him depressed. And, now he kinda' missin' all those phonies he use' to hang wit'.

⊷ Themes 'n' Shit ⊶

BEIN' LONELY AS FUCK

Erryone 'round Holden always rollin' fake. He try to connect wit' 'em anyway. But erry time he do, it end with Holden gettin' all towe up. This is one of da biggest reasons Holden always actin' out and hatin' on errything (130).

As real as Holden keep it, his teach Mr. Antolini keep it even **realer** and say, "Chin up, thug, you sho as hell ain't the only kid who ever felt lonely. So open up dem ears, playboy" (189).

TRYN'A FIGHT CHANGE

It's like Holden in a tug-of-war between youth and adulthood all throughout this book. He tryin' his damndest to keep it young, but fool gettin' his ass dragged to da adult side, and they ain't nothin' he can do 'bout it.

Sadly, no matter what this thug do, he ain't gonna win da battle against agin'. Matter of fact, dat point represented by Holden's gray hairs, which he dun had since he was a kid (9).

Even tho he rollin' like a geezer **physically**, he still actin' a **mental** fool, like he tryn'a stop time. But no matter how hard you hustlin', **nobody** gonna win da battle wit' time. Dat's one of da reasons Holden always tellin' adults where they can stick it, and would rather chill wit' little kids instead.

In fact, one of da few times Holden feelin' right is when he peepin' his sista, Phoebe, goin' 'round and 'round on da carousel— "I felt so damn happy all of a sudden. . . . I was damn near bawling. . . . I don't know why" (213).

And like a carousel dat go round and round, Holden wanna keep repeatin' his childhood over and over again, and delay adulthood for as long as he can.

DA CATCHER IN DA RYE

One of da thangs that pop up over and over is dat homies always be fallin' and disappearin':

Allie, don't let me disappear. Allie, don't let me disappear. Allie, don't let me disappear. Please, Allie. (198)

It was that kind of crazy afternoon. . . . You felt like you were disappearing every time you crossed a road. (5)

But you know what? Dat's jus' a part of growin' up, yo: losin' pieces of yo'self. Da older you get, da more tough decisions da world gonna force you to make. A lot of those decisions mean you gonna compromise yo'self and yo' ideals over and over again, until dat "pure and innocent child" you once were is looooong gone.

This is why Holden callin' himself the **Catcher in the Rye**—cuz he tryn'a save all da otha kids from fallin' off da cliff into da world of adults.

> I keep picturing all these little kids playing some game in this big field of rye and all. Thousands of little kids, and nobody's around—nobody big, I mean—except me. And I'm standing on the edge of some crazy cliff. What I have to do, I have to catch everybody if they start to go over the cliff—I mean if they're running and they don't look where they're going I have to come out from somewhere and *catch* them. That's all I'd do all day. I'd just be the catcher in the rye and all. (173)

He don' want dem kids to lose they innocence and turn into a buncha fake-ass adults.

ROLLIN' FAKE

Like I been sayin'—people frontin' day in day out is one of da thangs dat make Holden hate da world around him so much. Das why it so damn hard for Holden to connect wit' people, and why he ain't trip-pin' when they kick him out of school. Fuckin' phonies errywhere, mayne (13).

Matter of fact, fool cain't even catch a movie without a buncha phonies trippin' up his game. Da whole time dat Holden's watchin' a flick, he's sweatin' dat da actors are gonna fuck up and do somethin' phony (116–117).

✦ SPARKY'S CLASSROOM ✦

Greek derivation of da English word "Hypocrite"
Da English word "hypocrite" come from ancient Greek, and was da word used for what we now call an actor. Literally, it meant "one who responds." But by extension, da word come to mean one who responds wit' a buncha bullshit, or wit' somethin' actively contradictin' somethin' else they are or say.

GETTIN' IT ON

On da one hand, Holden always bitchin' 'bout horny bro-types treatin' girls like shit and still get-tin' dat nookie, like his roomie Stradlater. Holden even smacks him in his grill when he won't fess up to fuckin' Jane (43).

But on da otha hand, dat fool Holden a horndog himself. If he ain't mackin' hoodrats in the local bar or dialin' back-when bitches, he gettin' himself a prostitute. But you know what's real crazy? Fool never goes through wit' it. Cuz gettin' balls-deep in muff only gonna make him more adult, naw mean?

✌ Images 'n' Symbols ✌

BASEBALL MITT

Holden got his heart fucked up when his lil bro, Allie, died. And one of da thangs dat always remind him of Allie is dat little fool's baseball mitt. All Holden's jabberin' 'bout it not only give us insight into Holden's pain and mental state but also serve to fo'shadow his desire to be da catcher in the rye, since a baseball playa gotta wear a mitt. Holden might not have been able to do shit to save his brutha from leukemia, but he sho as hell gonna try savin' little kids from havin' to deal with the fake-ass world of adults (38–39).

DUCKS AND DA MUSEUM

One symbol of Holden's beef wit' life's inevitable changes is how he constantly wonderin' 'bout dem ducks in Central Park: "Do you happen to know where they go, the ducks, when it gets all frozen over?" (60)

What Holden want da most is for errything to stay da same, exactly how it is. As time pass, tho, seasons change, one homie leaves, and anotha arrives.

In da same vein, all da dummies in da museum are stiff as fuck and don't change . . . jus' da way Holden like it:

> The best thing, though, in that museum was that everything always stayed right where it was. Nobody'd move. . . . Nobody'd be different. The only thing that would be different would be *you*. (121)

RED HAT

First off, Holden put his hunting cap on backward like catchers do in a baseball game: "I swung the old peak way around to the back" (18).

But it ain't jus' cuz he lookin' fly like dat; it also showin' dat this fool **don't give a fuck** 'bout da way thangs should be. He gonna stick it to da man like a true-blue G.

Da hat also symbolizin' two different sides of Holden:

On one hand, da catcher in the rye wanna save people. But on da otha hand, **it's a huntin' hat**, so it also expressin' da part of Holden dat **hate** most of da people he gotta deal wit'. Brutha even go as far as to call it a people-shooting hat (52). **Word?**

⮾ Shout-Outs! ⮾

Givin' props to otha works dat preachin' da same truths as *The Catcher in the Rye*.

Classic

ACHILLES: I hate like the gates of Hades the man who says one thing and holds another in his heart.

—Homer, *Iliad*

REMIX

Even ancient Greek heroes were hatin' on phonies! You in good company, Holden!

✦ ✦ ✦

Classic

When a child first catches adults out—when it first walks into his grave little head that adults do not always have divine intelligence, that their judgments are not always wise, their thinking true, their sentences just—his world falls into panic desolation. The gods are fallen and all safety gone. And there is one sure thing about the fall of gods: they do not fall a little; they crash and shatter or sink deeply into green muck. It is a tedious job to build them up again; they never quite shine. And the child's world is never quite whole again. It is an aching kind of growing.

—John Steinbeck, *East of Eden*

REMIX

As soon as Holden realize how jacked-up and broken adults be, his whole world start to look real different.

✦ ✦ ✦

Classic

If one's different, one's bound to be lonely.

—Aldous Huxley, *Brave New World*

REMIX

Holden don't see da world like otha folk do; he don't act like they act, and he don't talk how they talk. Yeah, there are peeps who got his back; but what he really want is to find somebody who can be by his side.

✦ ✦ ✦

Classic

First thing I wanted to know,
what's the reason he dead?

—Jay Z, "A Dream"

REMIX

Po' Holden jus' cain't get over losin' his bro Allie.

Crime and Punishment

So What's the Deal?

$C+P$ ain't written by jus' any ol' scrub who think he know somethin' 'bout dodgin' da law. This book written by one of da bleakest, realest, and most philosophical cats in da Russian lit game: Fyodor Dostoevsky (da otha big dawg bein' my man Lev Nikolaevich Tolstoy). Not only do Fyodor got his own statue up in St. Petersburg, but this brutha wrote da first existentialist book before da word "existentialism" even **existed**. Man. Dat's gangsta.

Over a hundred years afta Dostoevsky was doin' his thang, smartass homies in literature, philosophy, and cinema name-dropping this playa on da reg: like Jean-Paul Sartre, Sigmund Freud, Woody Allen, and Alfred Hitchcock.

Crime and Punishment don't only spit fly rhymes 'bout morality, suffering, and religion, but it also a balls-to-the-wall **thrilla**!

Most mysteries always askin' da same question: "Who da killa?" But *Crime and Punishment* different. We **know** who da killa be. Da real drama comin' from da war goin' on in Raskolnikov's dome. Is Raskolnikov's theory tight? Are some playas thuggin' **so** righteous dat they got da **right** to kill somebody?

Homies

RODION ROMANOVICH RASKOLNIKOV (RODYA)

Like most twentysomethin's, Rodya jus' got outta school and now he broke as shit wit' no job. Brutha **mad** smart, tho. Back in da day, he wrote an article philosophizin' dat some peeps so special dat they got da **right** to kill somebody for da greater good. But once he put his money where his mouth is and ice two women, he spend da whole novel tweakin' **out**.

SOFYA SEMYONOVNA MARMELADOV (SONYA)

A pasty-ass girl who gotta turn tricks on da street to support her family. Girl been shit on her whole life, but she ain't trippin' 'bout it. She religious as fuck, and jus' glad to have dat gangsta Jesus lookin' out for her. When shit gets raw for Raskolnikov, Sonya don't judge. Instead, she jus' want him to get back to sippin' dat Jesus joose.

ALYONA IVANOVNA

A pawnbroker who notorious in da hood for bein' a stank bitch. All she do is smack up her sweet sista, Lizaveta, fuck people over, and stack paper jus' to count it. Raskolnikov thinkin': "Man, wouldn't da hood be a betta place wit'out this hag?"

Thug Life

LIZAVETA IVANOVNA

Da pawnbroker's lil sista. When she ain't buryin' her face in a copy of da Bible, her sista bossin' her 'round like she **own** her or somethin'. Nuh-uh, girl. Cain't be doin' dat. She also pretty cool with Sonya, and is da reason dat Sonya cruisin' down dat righteous path of God.

PORFIRY PETROVICH

Da hella smart cop who headin' up da investigation of Alyona's an' Lizaveta's murders. Porfiry read Rodya's article "Concerning Crime," an' he da only pig who know Rodya capable of doin' somethin' whack as mercin' two biddies. Porfiry mad-doggin' Rodya 24/7 tryn'a get him to fess up. This dude good cop AND bad cop.

AVDOTYA ROMANOVNA RASKOLNIKOV (DUNYA)

Raskolnikov's sexy sista. She got mad love for her bro, an' cuz of dat, she 'bout to shack up wit' some rich stiff named Luzhin jus' to hook Rodya up wit' a cushy job. But soon as Luzhin start talkin' smack 'bout her family, Dunya drop his ass **cold**.

ARKADY IVANOVICH SVIDRIGAILOV

Dunya used to be this dude's maid. Fool got it so bad for her, dat he ready to do almost anythin' to get some of dat sweet hunny-love.

DMITRI PROKOFICH RAZUMIKHIN

Raskolnikov's homeboy from school. A true-blue friend who always got his boy's back, Razumikhin gonna make sure Dunya and her mama ain't takin' shit from nobody while Raskolnikov off doin' his thang. Truth is, he want a lil slice of Dunya's pie too.

✒ What Went Down? ✒

Rodion Romanovich Roskalnikov—or Rodya, as he known on da streets—is one of da baddest white boys in da Western-lit game. Brutha livin' broke-as-a-joke in da hood of St. Petersburg. Even tho he a student, he don't seem to be doin' much studyin'. Most of da time he cruisin 'round town to get psyched up for some mysterious deed he plannin'.

One day, Raskolnikov walk up to da house of a notorious pawn-broker named Alyona to slang some of his bling for dat rent money. But he ain't only there to get some ends. He also scopin' da place out. **What this fool plannin'?** Afta dat crusty bag do my boy straight dirty by givin' him pennies for his goods, he go to get his drank on. While he sippin' on some Henny, mindin' his own bidness, a piss-drunk cat named Marmeladov start spillin' his guts. Marmy talkin' 'bout how his useless drunk-ass so damn cashed-out that his daughter, Sonya, gotta turn tricks on da street jus' so da family can make ends meet.

Lata, Rodya head up to Marmeladov's crib wit' him. Afta seein' Marmeladov's wife lay a whoop on his bitch ass, Rodya start feelin' all bad and toss da fam some dolla' billz before he leave.

Next day, Roskalnikov get a letter from his mama sayin' she and his lil sista, Dunya, 'bout to drop into town. Apparently, Dunya's fine-ass-self been workin' as a maid in da crib of some creeper name Svidrigailov. But when he tried to slide a couple fingers down da crack of Dunya's ass, Dunya said, "Exit only, bitch," and got da fuck outta there.

Now dat she outta dat situation, she plannin' to marry some rich lawyer named Pyotr Luzhin thinkin' maybe he can hook Rodya up with a job. Then Raskolnikov start thinkin': "Maybe my lil sista only hoppin' up on this fool's dick jus' to help me out?" Well **fuck** that. Rasky don't need none of dat, and say: Chari-**deez nuts**!

Afta havin' some jacked-up dream 'bout a horse gettin' the beat-down of its life, Raskolnikov strollin' through town when he peep game at da pawnbroker's sista, Lizaveta. He listen in on her convo and find out da pawnbroker gonna be all alone tomorrow. Aw shit, son—**perfect** time to roll up on dat hag.

So Rodya step up, grab himself an axe, cruise down to da pawnbroker's spot, and **pop pop**, dat bitch goes **down**! Jus' when Rodya 'bout to bail, her sista, Lizaveta, stroll in. Oh snap! Rodya decide in a flash dat he gotta keep it stone-cold gangsta and stack anotha body. So **pop**, Lizaveta gets an axe to the freakin' **face**. She dead.

Rodya get his ass home and next thang he know, boy straight **tweakin'**—lookin' all up in his clothes for bloodstains and actin' paranoid. He hides all dem phat stacks from da pawnbroker's stash underneath a stone, and then proceeds to pass da fuck out. Thankfully, his boy Razumikhin lookin' out for his ass, and try to get him back on his feet.

Afta 'bout five days, some uppity-lookin' dude name Luzhin roll in—dat same dick-slap tryn'a put a ring on Raskolnikov's sista, Dunya. Raskolnikov diss Luzhin real good, and he storms out all butt-hurt.

Raskolnikov finally head outta the crib, and he see dat drunk ol' Marmeladov got his ass run over by a horse. Now fool is bleedin' errywhere and makin' a goddamn mess. So Raskolnikov take Marmeladov home where he die in his daughter Sonya's arms. It such a sad sight dat Rasknolnikov leave 'em a stack of twenty rubles—all da change he got in da world. Killa wit' a heart of gold.

Lata, Rodya and Razumikhin head ova to da po-lice station to pick up some of da bling dat Rodya sold to da pawnbroker back when. Rodya s'posed to act normal, but when they get there, Rodya start laughin' like he **on** something. **Man, play it cool!**

Porfiry start playin' all kinda mind games with Rodya, and then pull out the **big guns**:

He say he read an article dat Rodya wrote called "Concerning Crime." In it, Rodya doin' some real raw philosophizin': he say there are ballas swingin' such big dicks dat they got da right to kill for da sake of a greater good.

CONCERNING
CRIME
~ BY ~
Rodion Romanovich Raskolnikov

Some homies so legit, they can kill for the good of the hood.

Next day, Raskolnikov wake up to see some nasty old dude name Svidrigailov all up in his grill. Apparently, this dat cat who Dunya use to work for, who was tryn'a get in her panties. So Svidrgailov say, "Look, bruh, I'm obsessed wit' dat ass. You wanna help a brutha out?" Raskolnikov tell him where to stick it, and Svidrigailov get his creepy ass outta there.

Lata, Raskolnikov chillin' with Razumikhin and da fam when Luzhin show up and start actin' like a punk. Dunya say, "Man, fuck you and yo' phat pockets," an' drop da engagement then 'n' there.

Then Rodya pay Sonya a visit. She tell him she used to be tight wit' Lizaveta, who showed her the Good Word of Christ. Raskolnikov ask her to read him da story of Lazarus, and she oblige a brutha.

Next day, Rodya drop in at the po-lice station when Porfiry be all like, "Rodya! Stop frontin', man. I know it was you who killed dem bitches!" Jus' when Rodya 'bout to crack, a painter name Nikolai bust in and confess to da murders. Porfiry don't believe a damn word Nikolai say, but has to let Rodya off da hook. Damn, dat was close.

Afta seein' Sonya deal with some whack shit at her daddy's funeral, Raskolnikov go up to her room and break it down: He killed Lizaveta and her crusty sista. But not cuz he needed da dough, cuz he wanted to prove dat he could—dat he was more than yo average homie.

Sonya say, "Goddamn, B! You okay? Shit like dat would jack up a brutha real good. If I was you, I'd turn my ass into da po-lice and beg God for forgiveness!"

Lata, Porfiry Petrovich hit up Ro-deezy one las' time to say, "Look, dog, even tho dat fool Nikolai takin' da heat, I **know** it was you. I can prove it too, so you might as well fess up." Rodya shake dat hata off and get back to bidness.

Shit gets weird when Svidrigailov corners Dunya and start layin' it on thick. But Dunya don't play dat game. She whip out a piece and say, "Back the fuck off, whody!" Svidrigailov finally get da hint she'll never want him, and let her go. Then he go outside, load up his piece, and pop one in his own head. Damn.

Afta confessin' to Dunya, Raskolnikov hit up Sonya for one more Bible sesh before he turn himself into da law. Then he go to da middle of da market, bow down in front of a shit-ton of folk, and kiss da ground to ask for they forgiveness. Las' of all, he roll up to da fuzz and confess.

For his punishment, Rodya get sent to cold-as-a-bitch Siberia. Only da gnarly sufferin' of prison life can bring him da redemption he need. Wit' Sonya at his side, Rodya finally realize dat it ain't bein' next-level dat gonna save his life. Naw, B—it only **love** dat can raise us from da dead.

ᨀ Themes 'n' Shit ᨀ

JUS' ANOTHA COG IN DA MAN MACHINE?

Raskolnikov pushin' dat murderous philosophy of his cuz it straight-up **logical**: if a special brutha jus' need to choke a bitch or two for da greater good, why not do it?

> For one life taken, thousands saved from corruption and decay! One death, and a hundred lives in exchange—why, it's simple arithmetic! (56)

It's simple arithmetic!

But afta goin through all sortsa shit and gettin' learned by Sonya, he realize dat livin' in a world full of homies who jus' logical and materialistic gonna create a real shitty place: if you thinkin' that all there be is logic, then we ain't really got any choice in what we do, which mean we don't gotta take responsibility for shit—so bruthas can backstab, cheat, steal, and ain't nobody gotta ride the beef.

So, you could look at Dostoevsky's book as a big fuck-you to a world that's straight-up logical. See, Raskolnikov thought he wouldn't break a sweat icin' peeps, since his reason for doin' it is rational. But when Raskolnikov loses his shit, he sees dat life is more than jus' an equation you can solve by crunchin' numbers.

THINKIN' YOU ABOVE DA LAW

✦ SPARKY'S CLASSROOM ✦

Da Übermensch, or Superman, is a concept by Freidrich Nietzsche, one of da most gangsta philosophers of all time. It's basically da next step in man's evolution.

Years before da German philosophizer Friedrich Nietzsche was rappin' 'bout a ultimate badass who acts on principles beyond good and evil, or "the Superman," Dostoyevsky was goin' off 'bout similar shit. Raskolnikov's article "Concerning Crime" theorizes dat some special playas got da **moral right** to do what they gotta do for da good of da world—even if it mean killin' somebody (220). Errything's permitted—even murder.

There are two kinds of hoods: Yo' regulah erryday scrubs who jus' doin' what erryone else tell 'em to do. And then there the ones who got da brains and balls to bring they own big ideas to life. Raskolnikov thinkin' he one of these special playaz, and dat's why he kills dat crusty hag.

EXCEPTIONAL PEOPLE THROUGHOUT HISTORY

JULIUS CAESAR   NAPOLEON   RASKOLNIKOV   JAY Z

Matta of fact, ol' Raskolnikov thinkin' his only REAL crime was fuckin' up and confessin'. It wasn't killin' a hag dat was wrong, but thinkin' he special when he ain't: "This was the sole sense in which he acknowledged his crime, that he had not succeeded and that he had confessed" (459).

THINKIN' VS. DOIN'

Even tho Raskolnikov been throwin' 'round da idea of errything bein' permitted—even murder—it ain't so easy to put yo' money where yo' mouth is. Talkin' 'bout killin' a brutha is one thang, but actually steppin' up, pumpin' a clip, and rainin' bullets on someone is a whole otha game, yo. Like Raskolnikov say, "That's why I don't act, because I am always talking. Or perhaps I talk so much just because I can't act" (2).

ERRYDAY I'M SUFFERIN'

Yeah, sufferin' can suck a fat one, no doubt. But to some playas, like Raskolnikov, sufferin' ain't somethin' to be avoided—it's straight-up necessary if you wanna be a real G. Like Raskolnikov say:

> Suffering and pain are always obligatory on those of wide intellect and profound feeling. Truly great men must, I think, experience great sorrow on the earth. (224)

At first, our boy think he da numba one stunna, but refuse to suffer. But then at da end he realize sufferin' is where it's **at** cuz it's da only thang dats gonna redeem him of his twisted-ass deeds. But now dat he's embraced suffering, does dat mean he **actually is** one of da great few? Dostoevsky dun mind-fucked us.

✌ Images 'n' Symbols ✌

SONYA'S CROSS

Rasknolikov start off thinkin' he can handle errything on his own, but he come to see dat this world can put more on yo' shoulders than even the hardest soulja can bear. So ol' Rodya hit up Sonya to lighten da load. And if one person in *C+P* knows 'bout bruthas needin' to let off a load, it's Sonya (11).

In fact, for Raskolnikov, she's got so much pain to grind through that she like a symbol for all da suffering in da world (272–273). Girl puts herself on da streets so she can bring home da cheddar to a starvin' family; and instead of her pops lendin' a hand, he jus' drinks and gets his ass kicked by a goddamn horse.

Raskolnikov hit up Sonya so she'll ease summodat suffering. But for a little while, she actually make him suffer **more** in order for God to forgive him. Greater sufferin' gives Rodya new life. So in a lotta ways, Sonya's sufferin' is pretty damn Christ-like. As Rodya take a cross from Sonya, he say, "This, then, is a symbol that I am taking up my cross. . . . As if my earlier sufferings had been mere trifles!" (442)

RESURRECTION AND THE BIBLICAL LAZARUS

First time Rodya chill wit' Sonya one on one, she crack open a copy of da Bible and lay down da story of Lazarus.

Who dat? Three days afta his death, Lazarus is brought back to life by Jesus. Afta seein' this, ain't nobody in da hood doubt that JC was da real deal.

Jus' like Lazarus was brought back to life through his belief in da big Jay C, Rodya is saved by da good work of Sonya, who always schoolin' him on redemption through Christ. It's like he reborn. Naw mean? Dude falls at her feet, grabs her knees, and starts cryin':

> In their white sick faces there glowed the dawn of a new future, a perfect resurrection into a new life. Love had raised them from the dead, and the heart of each held endless springs of life for the heart of the other. (463)

Dostoevsky even droppin' lil baby hints of **mo'** Lazarus imagery. See, Jesus tell his posse they gotta move a stone outta the way of a cave before Lazarus can be reborn.

Likewise, Rodya ain't gonna be forgiven for shit (reborn) 'til he prove dat he killed dem two ladies. So he roll back dat stone to show da fuzz where he was stashin' da pawnbroker's goods.

DA NAME "RASKOLNIKOV"

Raskolnikov's name got roots in da word "raskol," which mean "schism," highlightin' one of da main motifs up in here: Shit bein' divided like finely cut yeyo.

✦ SPARKY'S CLASSROOM ✦

Schism: division or disunion, especially into mutually opposcd partics.

First off, Raskolnikov's mind always divided 'bout who he really be. In da beginnin', fool think he an ice-cold killa who can do whateva he damn well please. But eventually, he recognize dat ain't da case. Like Prokofich say 'bout Rodion: "It is as if he had two separate personalities each dominating him alternately" (182).

Sometime Rodya cain't stand bein' 'round people. Then otha times, he cain't get enough of 'em. Sometime, he act like he don't give a fuck 'bout nobody, but otha times we hear 'bout him saving kids from burning buildings and he even pays for Marmeladov's funeral. Consistency ain't this fool's strong suit.

RASKOLNIKOV'S DREAMS

Raskolnikov has some trippy-ass dreams, man. He musta smoked a blunt or two before he went to bed, cuz Rodya dreamin' dat he a lil-ass thug watchin' a horse gettin' whupped by its owner (47–48).

Dat ol' horse gettin' a beatdown from its owner could stand for all sortsa shit—

+ Raskolnikov see himself as da peasant, which mean he subconsciously recognizin' dat he ain't da great man he thinkin' he be.
+ Dat peasant got da moral **right** to lay a whoop on dat horse since it's his own damn property. Likewise, Rodya think he got da moral **right** to merc da pawnbroker and her sista cuz he such a G.
+ Da whole dream reppin' Sonya. Sonya takin' on all this suffering jus' like dat horse. Plus, her daddy was run over by one.

And if you wanna get *real* cray, Raskolnikov's dream when he sick in Siberia gonna make you need to change yo tighty-whities:

He had dreamt in his illness that the whole world was condemned to fall. . . . They did not know how or whom to judge and could not agree what was evil and what good. . . . They thrust and cut, they killed and ate one another. . . . The plague grew and spread wider and wider. In the whole world only a few could save themselves, a chosen handful of the pure, who were destined to found a new race of men and a new life, and to renew and cleanse the earth; but nobody had ever seen them anywhere, nobody had heard their voices or their words." (461)

This dream talkin' 'bout what gonna happen to the world if errybody got the same philosophy dat Raskolnikov preachin' in his article: If we thinkin' we got da moral right to do whateva we want to *whomever* we want, then this world gonna end in a shit storm of chaos. No thanks, son.

✐ Shout-Outs! ✐

Givin' props to otha works dat preachin' da same truths as *Crime and Punishment*.

Classic

Zeus had led us on to know,
the Helmsman lays it down as law
that we must suffer, suffer into truth.

—Aeschylus, *Agamemnon*

REMIX

To some, real sufferin' is a helluva lot mo' than jus' a pain in yo' ass: it's God-given **and** one of da only ways—maybe **da only way**—dat a playa can know real truth. I'm talkin' wisdom, son. Wit'out Rodya fuckin' peoples day up wit his axe, fool never would've found Jesus.

✦ ✦ ✦

Classic

I think man will never renounce real suffering, that is, destruction and chaos. Why, suffering is the sole origin of consciousness.
—Fyodor Dostoevsky, *Notes from Underground*

REMIX

True sufferin' can teach a thug da most important kinda knowledge: knowledge of himself and da world 'round him. And here's da craziest shit of all: dat knowledge **so dank** dat people **could never give up sufferin'**. I mean, Rodya marinated on wreckin' peeps for a loooong-ass time, and was certain he could go through wit' murder wit'out trippin'. We know how dat turned out . . .

✦ ✦ ✦

Classic

One must test oneself to see whether one is destined for independence and command; and one must do so at the proper time. One should not avoid one's tests, although they are perhaps the most dangerous game one could play and are in the end tests which are taken before ourselves and no other can judge.
—Friedrich Nietzsche, *Beyond Good and Evil*

REMIX

Rodya was damn sure he could roll deep wit' ballas like Napoleon and Solon—doin' dirty deeds for da good of da hood. But when Rodya finally man up and put his theory to da test, he get da **real** answers to questions he been askin'.

Things Fall Apart

✑ So What's the Deal? ✑

Now it don't take no schola to know dat imperial colonialism put da serious hurt on Africa's people and culture. And Chinua Achebe, da author of this fine piece, came up in a colonial society; so he knew firsthand da kinda damage done when peeps thinkin' one idea or culture betta than anotha.

But instead of jus' shamin' white peeps for comin' in, markin' turf dat ain't theirs, and fuckin' shit up in general—Chinua take it a step further. Yea, imperialism hella messed up. Ain't no doubt 'bout dat. But life in Africa—and anywhere else, for dat matta'—wadn't **all** gravy neitha. So even tho Achebe's main jam preachin' dat colonial attitudes are stone-cold killas, he spittin' anotha righteous truth: Ain't nothin' perfect. Some-way, somehow, errything gonna fall apart.

shiiiii...

∾ Homies ∾

OKONKWO

One of da honchos of his village Umuofia, and main playa of da book.
He always showin' out to prove he tougher than any otha thug on
da block, cuz to him, bein' a hard-ass warrior is what make a man a
man. Okonkwo's daddy wadn't nothin' but a lazy, cowardly bitch, so
Okonkwo hustlin' overtime to make up for dat family shame. Prollem
is, all his daddy issues make him go a lil too hard in da paint erry
now and again.

IKEMEFUNA

Okonkwo's adopted son who got snatched from anotha village.
Okonkwo and this lil kid got mad love for each otha. But Okonkwo
don't wanna show his feelin's, cuz love is for sensitive bitches. Sucks
for Ikemefuna—cuz of Okonkwo's need to swing a big dick 24/7,
Daddy end up helpin' to ice him.

NWOYE

Okonkwo's legit son. Nwoye ain't got a stick up his ass like Okonkwo
do. He like to kick back and keep thangs chill. Okonkwo ain't feelin'
him on dat, so he always whoopin' on him to toughen him up. Nwoye
real quick to convert to Christianity once da white people come to
town flossin' they fancy swag. Okonkwo ain't too cool wit' dat neitha.

OGBUEFI EZEUDU

One of da most respected elders in all Umuofia. This fool got certified
street cred by puttin' a buncha fools six feet deep back in da day.

Ogbuefi try to do Okonkwo a few solids by givin' him good advice, like, "Don't kill yo' adopted boy," but Okonkwo ain't always listen. Ironically, Okonkwo gonna not only ignore Ezeudu but kill his son too.

OBIERIKA

Okonkwo's main man, who look afta his shit while he exiled in dat trap Mbanta. Unlike most peeps in da tribe, Obierika ain't down wit' all da Umuofian ways. This playa think deep, and he jus' 'bout da only one who recognize dat some of dem Umuofian customs straight-up whack.

UNOKA

Okonko's no-good daddy who got a rep for bein' a weak, poor scrub. What a bitch.

✥ What Went Down? ✥

Okonkwo got a pretty sweet life up in da Nigerian village of Umuofia. He got mo' paper than most, he one of they baddest muthafuckin' warriors, and jus' 'bout erryone give him mad respect. Thang is, tho, his daddy, Unoka, wadn't nothin' but a broke-ass scrub always blowin' cash fast and tossin' back too much drank.

So Okonkwo gotta act like he da strongest, hardest thug in da village to show all dem haterz dat he ain't useless like his daddy. But this brutha might be takin' it too far, cuz erry now and again, he actin' a real dick to his wife and kids.

When da Umuofians catch word dat one of they girls got iced in da village of Mbaino, it look like there gonna be all-out war in da streets. Da otha tribe, tho, make peace by offerin' up a virgin and a fifteen-year-ol' lil G named Ikemefuna. Okonkwo end up takin' Ikemefuna under his roof, and Ikemefuna get real right wit' Okonkwo's son, Nwoye. Okonkwo thinkin' this kid so damn legit dat he let Ikemefuna call him "father." But even tho Ikemefuna make Okonkwo get all emotional and shit, Okonkwo too much of a gangsta to show it. Cain't be no weak-ass chump, amirite?

As time go on, Okonkwo cain't keep his temper in check and end up comin' out waaaaay too hard. Even tho it almost time for da New Yam Festival, when erryone supposed to jus' chill and pass da peace pipe, Okonkwo end up whoopin' one of his woman's ass jus' cuz she fucked up his banana tree boostin' some leaves. Afta she catch dat beatdown, she talk a little smack 'bout Okonkwo. Dat fool decide to step up his asshole-game, whip out his piece, and try to pop a cap in dat same woman. Trashy shit right there, Okonkwo.

One day, a respected ol' geezer named Ezeudu bring word from da Oracle: Even tho Ikemefuna been keepin' it trill up in Umuofia for three years, dude gotta die.

When Ezeudu break da news to Okonkwo, he say, "Look, bruh, you don't wanna ride da beef for dat. Keep yo' ass at home and jus' light one up. Afta all, da lil kid call you daddy." Shame to say, but Okonkwo don't follow Ezeudu's advice. Instead, Okonkwo and his villager homies tell Ikemefuna dat they gonna escort him back to Mbaino. When Okonkwo and his crew out in da middle of nowhere, some of da Umuofians whip out they blades and start attackin' Ikemefuna. Ikemefuna like, "**Oh shit!!**" and run toward Okonkwo screamin', "**Daddy, help!**" But Okonkwo keep it cold-blooded, whips out his shiv, and **ends** dat fool.

Okonkwo lata hit up his main brutha, Obierika, who like, "Damn,

Okonkwo! Dafuq you **thinkin'**? Ain't **nobody** s'posed to shed blood of they blood. Mother Earth ain't down wit' dat mess, and she wipe out whole families for fuck-ups like dat."

Not too much lata, Okonkwo and his fam get **hosed**. See, dat geezer Ezeudu bite da big one, and da village gonna put on a swagged-out funeral since he was such a righteous balla. Okonkwo helpin' pay homage to this dead homie wit' a Glock-salute: but when Okonkwo fire his piece, damn thang explodes and put a chunk of iron into da heart of Ezeudu's sixteen-year-ol' son! Didn't see dat comin'.

To da Umuofians, sheddin' clansman blood piss off da earth goddess real bad. So Okonkwo gotta take his fam and get da hell outta dodge. But da earth goddess ain't done there. Naw, playa. She got mo' justice to hand out: Okonkwo's old homies put on they war threads, burn down Okonkwo's house, and kill all his animals.

Okonkwo bring his wives and kids to Mbanta, his fo'real muthaland, where he get schooled by an old man name Uchendu. Afta a couple years of Okonkwo chillin' in Mbanta, Obierika swang into town to see what's what. And, he wanna tell Okonkwo 'bout da word on da street: Da village of Abame got wiped off da map.

Apparently, some white dude stepped on Abame's turf. Bad news for him, tho: When da elders of Abame hit up they Oracle, da Oracle tell 'em dat white dude jus' gonna shit in their tribal cereal. So da people of Abame strap up and put dat sucka down.

For a long time, ain't nothin' happen, til there was a big market in Abame. Three honkeys hit da town wit' a big-ass crew, surround da market, and go **pop pop**. Whole damn clan get wiped out like **dat**.

Two years pass, and Obierika come visit Okonkwo again. Turn out a buncha missionaries came to Umuofia and built churches errywhere. And da reason Obierika hit up Okonkwo is cuz his boy Nwoye is chillin' wit' dem holy rollers! Da hell?!

Obierika get da word on what went down before he visited Okonkwo: Dem missionaries had already cruised 'round Mbanta, and were tellin' errybody dat dem African gods ain't nothin' but a buncha fakers. Unless they wanna burn for all eternity, they best chunk deuce to they ol' gods and join up wit' JC's posse. Okonkwo thought they jus' talkin nonsense, but his son, Nwoye, ate dat shit up, and started chillin' wit' da Christian missionaries. When Okonkwo hear 'bout dat, he get so turnt up dat he grab Nwoye by da neck and beat his ass wit' a stick. Afta dat, his son peaces out for good.

Now dat Okonkwo's seven years of hard time in Mbanta is up, he head back to Umuofia where errything he once knew has gone to **shit**. Da white man taken over and most of Okonkwo's back-then homies have dropped they old religious grind and now sippin' on dat Jesus joose.

Okonkwo lookin' at his fellow Umuofians and like, "Man, wha's da deal wit' all deez honkies? And why you bitches jus' let 'em walk all over you and change shit? Pick up yo' nuts."

When some new missionary name of Smith come to town, he start layin' down da law all strict-like and don't respect none of da Umuofian customs. Lemme let Achebe get this one: "[Smith] saw things as black and white. And black was evil" (104).

Some shit goes down wit' Enoch, a converted tribal brutha. Fool literally commit one of da worst crimes anybody can in Umuofia: He unmask a *egwugwu* in public, basically shittin' on da worship of da earth goddess (105). Well, da Umuofians ain't havin' none of dat. Not only do they set Enoch's crib on fire, but they also burn Mr. Smith's church to da ground.

So da white man, real sneaky-like, call a meetin' of six Umuofian leaders, includin' Okonkwo. Next thang Okonkwo and his boys know, they jus' got they asses whooped and thrown in da big house. Then, da white folk make da whole damn village throw down some money to spring they leaders. Afta da village hand over some phat stacks, Okonkwo and da otha villagers hit da streets again and set up a meetin'. But when some honkies try to step up and tell errybody to get they asses home, Okonkwo loses his shit, steps up to da boss man, and **slices dat honkey's head off**. When he look 'round tho, he know it game over: instead of erryone takin' his back, ready to throw da white man outta town, they jus' whisperin' all scurred, "Why he do dat?" (116)

Lata, da Christians' district commissioner roll up to Okonkwo's compound to take him downtown to da slammer. He ask where Okonkwo be. Some villagers jus' say, "We gonna take you to him, and you can help some bruthas out." Da Commish find him, aight: Okonkwo's body hangin' from a tree. Turn out dat fool iced himself; and since da Umuofians see suicide as one of da biggest offenses against Mother Earth, none of da Umuofians can take his body down. Damn.

✎ Themes 'n' Shit ✎

THANGS FALLIN' APART (NO SHIT)

Up in this text, we seein' thangs fall apart in big ways and small ways. On a bigga level, da Igbo traditions comin' to an end cuz a whole buncha colonialist assholes strut in like they own da place. It's like they "put a knife on the things" dat hold all of Igbo culture together, and errything crumbles (100).

✦ SPARKY'S CLASSROOM ✦

"Dafuq is imperial colonialism?"
Basically it's when a nation roll up on somebody else's hood, claim it as they own, and start tellin' people dat they gotta live how they live and think how they think.

But on a smalla, mo' personal level, Okonkwo himself fallin' apart, and ultimately commit suicide. Like Obierika say at da end: "That man was one of the greatest men in Umuofia. You drove him to kill himself; and now he will be buried like a dog" (117).

SHAKIN' OFF DA SINS OF DA FATHER

Okonkwo 'shamed of his daddy cuz he was a lazy-ass good-for-nothin'. Since Okonkwo don't wanna be associated wit' such a bootleg rep, he usually comin' out **way too hard**. His daddy was also a pretty gentle brutha who never did no fightin', so Okonkwo gotta do da exact opposite and be a total hard-ass (10).

On da one hand, s'all good to Okonkwo, cuz erryone think he

successful from hustlin' so hard-core. But on da otha hand, it ain't so good cuz he ain't gonna show no emotions. He love Ikemefuna like a son, but love make you soft and Okonkwo ain't havin none of dat taintin' his rep. Okonkwo think dat "to show affection was a sign of weakness; the only thing worth demonstrating was strength" (18).

Da clan say ain't nobody gotta be trippin' 'bout da stupid shit they father did, cuz it ain't they fault. So in a way, da clan actin' all parental by protectin' peeps from da weak shit mommy and daddy (6–7).

At least, dat's how it's s'posed to be. But on da real, dat's a bunch of bullshit in practice—da whole reason dat Ikemefuna and his sis get shipped to Umuofia is cuz of somethin they pops did (9). No wonder shit fallin' apart.

GOTTA HAVE A COMMUNITY AT YO' BACK

There ain't no amount of sufferin' dat can't be beasted through wit' a lil help from yo' homies. When Okonkwo was comin' up from da streets, he had to hustle harder than ever, and conquerin' dat mess made him think he could survive anythin' (17).

But when you all alone, it's **way** worse: "It is more difficult and more bitter when a man fails *alone*" (17).

And dat one of the most important reasons dat Okonko kill himself: He feel like he da only one left who gonna fight for da old-school way of life.

HOMEBOY VS. HOMEGIRL

To Okonkwo, there ain't nothin' mo' important than bein' manly as fuck. Cuz to him, anythin' feminine is weak. But throughout da book, peeps gonna be tellin' him he gotta stop countin' his nut hairs and recognize dat da feminine side jus' as necessary. Sometime, even mo' so (74).

As big a badass as Okonkwo be, he thinkin' da only way you can

ball is wit' a set of balls. But Uchendu lay it
down for Okonkwo:

> Can you tell me, Okonkwo, why it is
> that one of the commonest names we
> give our children is Nneka, or "Mother
> is Supreme"? . . . Why is that? (77–78)

You gotta give props to da ladies.

⌇ Images 'n' Symbols ⌇

PALM KERNELS AND OIL

Now you might be thinkin': Dafuq is palm oil? Think of palm oil like
African hot sauce. You put it on grub to make it taste betta so you can
toss back dat nourishment. Well, da way peeps talkin' up in da novel
is like makin' food wit' palm oil:

> Among the Ibo the art of conversation is regarded very highly,
> and proverbs are the palm-oil with which words are eaten. (6)

This how da novel written too. Achebe didn't jot this shit down
in chronological order. Dude jump around when it gonna make da
story go down smoother. For example, at da end of chapter 2, Ikemefuna bein' ripped from da arms of his family, but instead of contin-
uin' on dat rhyme, chapter 3 start talkin' 'bout Okonkwo's father. We
don't even get back to da shit happenin' to Ikemefuna til chapter 4.

Speaking wit' palm oil is like a different kinda sweet-talkin'—one dat make shit easier to digest.

OKONKWO HIMSELF

Even tho Okonkwo always gettin' crunk 'bout da changes happenin' to Igbo culture, sometimes he doin' thangs dat be completely against dem same traditions.

For example, when he lay a whoop on one of his womenses during da Week of Peace, Ezeani say dat he put da whole damn clan at risk for disrespectin' da earth goddess durin' Prime Chill-Time (20).

And when Okonkwo shootin' da shit wit' Obierika, Obierika call him out for mercin' Ikemefuna, who was like his own son, and endangerin' his whole family (40–41).

As Okonkwo tryn'a rally his gang to wreck whitey and save they culture, he ask 'em to do somethin' dat Umuofians ain't s'posed to do: kill they own people (115).

But he don't stop there. Da last thang dat Okonkwo eva do is also forbidden by Umuofian culture—killin yo'self:

> It is against our custom . . . It is an abomination for a man to take his own life. It is an offense against the Earth, and a man who commits it will not be buried by his clansmen. (117)

THE GANKING OF IKEMEFUNA

Okonkwo hate his bitch-ass father, but he all 'bout his adopted son Ikemefuna . . . even tho he end up mercin' him like a cold-blooded gangsta. There be some biblical parallels all up in hurr.

In Genesis 22, God hit up Abraham and tell him he gotz to kill his son, Isaac, in order to prove how faithful he be. Abe 'bout to go through wit' it, but God do him a solid and spare Isaac. But in this book, there ain't no savin'. Even tho Okonkwo sacrificin' his "son" to show respect for da Oracle and Umuofian beliefs, he also doin' it to pay respects to his personal god: manliness, strength, and achievement (35, 38):

> He heard Ikemefuna cry, "My father, they have killed me!" as he ran towards him. Dazed with fear, Okonkwo drew his machete and cut him down. He was afraid of being thought weak. (38)

OKONKWO'S EXPLODING PIECE

Dat gun be a powerful reminder: Shit happen dat even da strongest hustla cain't control. Okonkwo thinkin' he all tight cuz he a self-made man and errybody all up on his nuts cuz he successful. But dat gun remind him dat street cred ain't errything.

> But although Okonkwo was a great man whose prowess was universally acknowledged, he was not a hunter. In fact he had not killed a rat with his gun. (24–25)

Fool can't kill what he tryn'a kill, but he do end up accidentally killing Ezeudu's boy (74).

FIRE

Okonkwo's name on da streets is "Roaring Flame." Fool got a fiery temper and he often associated wit' flame throughout da novel: "Okonkwo's fame had grown like a bush-fire in the harmattan" (3).

But this ain't necessarily a good thang. Fire wreck errything in its path and leave nothin' but ash.

> He was a flaming fire . . . And immediately Okonkwo's eyes were opened and he saw the whole matter clearly. Living fire begets cold, impotent ash. (89)

Cashed.

⚬ Shout-Outs! ⚬

Givin' props to otha works dat preachin' da same truths as *Things Fall Apart*.

Classic

> I imagined leave would be different from this. Indeed, it was different a year ago. It is I of course that have changed in the interval. There lies a gulf between that time and to-day. At that time I still knew nothing about the war, we had only been in quiet sectors. But now I see that I have been crushed without knowing it. I find I do not belong here any more, it is a foreign world.
>
> —Erich Maria Remarque, *All Quiet on the Western Front*

REMIX

Okonkwo been fightin' all his life, against otha peeps, da fear of endin' up like his pops, and finally—da change dat's overtakin' his turf and crew. Playa don't even recognize da world 'round him no mo'.

✦ ✦ ✦

Classic

> There comes a time when a man gets mad. . . . Them deputies— Did you ever see a deputy that didn' have a fat ass? An' they waggle their ass an' flop their gun aroun'. "Ma," he said, "if it was the law they was workin' with, why, we could take it. But it *ain't* the law. They're a-workin' away at our spirits. They're a-trin' to make us cringe an' crawl like a whipped bitch. They tryin' to break us. Why, Jesus Christ, Ma, they comes a time when the on'y way a fella can keep his decency is by takin' a sock at a cop."
>
> —John Steinbeck, *The Grapes of Wrath*

REMIX

Okonkwo knew damn well dat when da man try to roll up on **yo'** house flexin' like he da law, you jus' gotta say, "Fuck da po-lice."

✦ ✦ ✦

Classic

> But I ain't no politician, no competition
> Sending all oppositions to see a mortician.
>
> —Dr. Dre, "Keep Their Heads Ringin'"

REMIX

Okonkwo woulda been **real down** wit' Dre; you get in O's way, you gonna get buried.

The
Color
Purple

✦ ✛ ✦

✒ So What's the Deal? ✑

Listen up: Alice Walker's novel *The Color Purple* so hard-core dat it been puttin' folks draws in a bunch since it hit da streets in da early 1980s. In fact, peep da American Library Association's list of da 100 Most Frequently Challenged Books of 2000–2009—guess who made it to numba 17? Mmmm-hmmmm. Das' my girl!

See, a lot of dem real uptight folk usually flip shit cuz of da book's violence, bean-flickin', and incest. But lemme make this clear: Anybody keepin' othas from pickin' up this novel is a damn fool, straight up.

Walker's novel layin' down some real talk 'bout what it mean to love, hate, and forgive; and it hittin' dem high notes when it comes to self-acceptance, Christianity, family life, racism, and womanhood.

At da end of da day, yeah, this book got stuff dat'll prolly make a few homies uncomfortable, but tell 'em to grind through it anyway, so they can see (jus' like da big playas in da novel) dat we all connected; we all united. No matta what kinda shit we been through, da only thang dat gonna get us outta dat trap is love.

All dat to say: *The Color Purple* ain't jus' da color of my favorite weed I blowin' and drank I sippin'—it also one of da most throwed-up texts yo' bitch-ass ever gonna read.

❧ Homies ❧

CELIE

Girl been abused by men her whole damn life. Her "daddy" beat her and rape her on da reg. Sheeit, she even pop out two of his incest babies. Celie ain't educated, but she write up a goddamn storm. Word, sista. Spittin' dem flows help Celie beast through all dat bullshit gettin' dropped on her 24/7, but she still need a little somethin' else: the love of homegirl Shug Avery. Through Shug's sugar, Celie gonna learn how to break from da past, embrace love, and live life on her own damn terms. She spend most of da novel learnin' to love herself, to love othas, and tryn'a reunite wit' her sista. At da end of da book, this bad biddy finally get all three.

SHUG AVERY

A fly singah wit' an ass dat don't quit. Shug so fine dat jus' 'bout errybody she meet want a piece. In fact, she and Celie's husband use to have a lil somethin' somethin' on da side, which is why he bring Shug back to his crib when she sick. Celie end up takin' care of her, and at first, Shug act a straight-up bitch. But afta a while, they get tight. **Real tight.** Mmmmmmm-hmmmmm. Shug completely change da way Celie look at da world: She help

Celie see dat no matta what she been through, she—jus' like erry-body else—deserve some lovin'.

ALBERT (CALLED MR. ____ OR MISTER)

Celie's hubby who really wanted somebody else's ooo-wee but had to settle for second best—Celie; and he sure as hell make sure she know it. For years, Mister beat da hell outta Celie. He even keep from Celie one of da only thangs she really want: letters from her sista, Nettie. Truth is, Celie don't mean much of nothin' to Mister for a long-ass time, cuz all he can think 'bout is da one dat got away: Shug Avery. Late in da book tho, Mister recognize he been actin' a fool and start tryn'a keep it church.

NETTIE

Celie's younger and finer sista. At first, Mister wanna marry this dip, but her "father," Alphonso, wanna keep her all to his nasty-ass self. So Nettie say, "Fuck this shit," and run away from home, eventually endin' up wit' a couple of missionaries. Over da years, Nettie sendin' Celie letters on da reg, but Mister keep interceptin' 'em like a bitch. Afta mo' than thirty years, Nettie and Celie don't need no mo' letters: they get reunited. Hell yeah.

HARPO

Mister's oldest son, who tryn'a keep his woman in check wit' da back side of his hand, jus' like his daddy always do. But Harpo's wife jus' too big a badass to let him wear da pants in da relationship. Crazy thang is, Harpo only actin' like an asshole cuz he think he s'posed to. But on da real, he a pretty sensitive thug. Once Harpo chills wit' da whole "tryn'a be manly man" bullshit, he and Sofia can actually work they prollems out.

SOFIA

Harpo's girl who don't take no shit from nobody. She don't give a fuck. She'll punch men, otha women, her husband, even da mayor! Eventually all this back-talkin' get her trapped inta cleanin' da mayor's house for years, but still—she keep it real. This hustlah deserve major props for tellin' it like it is and fightin' against all da bullshit dat da world try to pile on her.

ALPHONSO

Celie and Nettie thinkin' this fool they daddy for a long time. But turn out, he ain't related to 'em by blood: he jus' scooped up dem kids to get his greedy-ass hands on they mama's phat stacks. Alphonso one backward-ass dude. He rape Celie all da time when she was a lil girl, makin' her pop out two babies, then stealin' em from her. This guy's a bitch, plain and simple.

～ What Went Down? ～

Life pretty much **suck** for lil girl Celie. We gettin' da beat on Celie's fucked-up life from a buncha letters she sendin' to God beggin' for change in her life.

So what she writin' da big G-man for anyway? Well, her "daddy," Alphonso, keep rapin' her like it ain't no thang, and already impregnate her once. Afta she had

da baby, her daddy swiped and prolly killed it . . . Celie know her daddy jus' ice-cold enough to do it. Now she preggers **again** wit' one of Alphonso's kidz. **Shit,** man! And to make mattas even worse, Celie's mama jus' died; but right before she kick da can, she went out cussin' and screamin' at Celie. Awesome.

At least Celie got her sista, Nettie—thang is, dat ain't gonna last too much longa neitha. Some hood name Albert (but Celie always jus' callin' him "Mister") say he wanna get himself summodat Nettie-sauce. But Alphonso don't want some otha scrub getting his grubby paws on his finest daughter, so he slang Celie his way instead and she marry him.

So Celie get outta one hellhole jus' to end up in anotha. On top of gettin' raped and beaten by Mister (man, what is **up** wit' deez people?), Celie also gotta take care of his lil-shit kids.

Lata, Nettie run away to join up wit' Celie at her new digs. Turn out dat Mister still wanna crack at dat ass, so he start tryn'a put da moves on Nettie again. Nettie ain't havin' none of dat, so Mister give her ass da boot. Before she go, Nettie say she gonna write Celie 24/7, but Celie never get a single letter. It ain't like Nettie to forget somethin' like dat, so Celie thinkin' she must be dead.

Years pass and Mister's kiddos leave da crib, 'cept for his boy Harpo. Harpo start layin' da mack down on a hunny name Sofia, and it ain't long before they married. Sofia come live wit' Harpo at Mister and Celie's spot, and she show errybody dat she one tough bitch. Errytime dat Harpo try to get crunk on Sofia, she keep it trill and put his hater-ass in check. Celie

If you wanna act like a bitch, I'm a treat ya like a bitch!

cain't believe how gangsta Sofia keepin' it, and actually get so jealous of Sofia dat she tell Harpo he need to lay down da law and pimp-slap a ho. Harpo try to do jus' dat, and end up gettin' his ass whooped.

When Sofia get all up in Celie's grill, askin' why she sold a sista out, Celie apologize and say she jus' wish she could fight back like Sofia do.

Not long afta dat, Mister's back-when bitch, name Shug Avery, get real sick and need a place to crash. So Mister has Shug set up shop in his crib, and Celie gonna look afta her. Shug don't pay Celie no real mind, and at first a real cold-ass bitch toward her; but Celie jus' can't take her eyes off Shug, and don't know why.

Eventually Sofia get tired of Harpo always tryn'a flex nuts, so she chunk deuce outta dat house. Well, playa's gonna play: Harpo get a new girlfriend named Squeak and open up a bar where Shug start singin'. When Shug find out dat Mister always layin' a whoop on Celie, she decide she gotta stay in dat house even tho she healthy now. Now Celie hotter for her than eva.

Then Sofia come back one day and get all up in Squeak's grill. **Cat fight, son!** Sofia pop dat bitch right in da mouth.

Prollem is, Sofia jus' don't know how to play it cool. She get in some trouble wit' da law for smackin' da mayor in da face afta his wife try to tell Sofia she **got** to be their maid. For actin' out like dat, Sofia get thrown in da big house. Thangs become cool between Squeak and Sofia when Squeak start carin' for her kids while she locked up. Squeak even try to blackmail da sheriff (her uncle) into lettin' Sofia go, but it don't work and da sherriff jus' rape her instead. Damn. Sofia get released and end up havin' to work as a maid afta all.

Shug peace out for a little while, but return to da hood wit' a new man in her life—a husband name Grady. Even tho she married, she still get buck wild wit' Celie. Afta doin da nasty, they start talkin 'bout Nettie. Shug like, "Oh shit, I seen Mister wit' a shit-ton of letters before." Apparently dat scrub been gettin' Nettie's letters, but hidin' 'em from Celie. Afta tearin' through all his shit, they eventually find da stash. Celie so pissed she could **kill** dat muthafucka.

Da letters say Nettie hooked up wit' some missionary couple, Samuel and Corrine, and she up in Africa wit' 'em slangin' good deeds. Not only dat, but turn out Celie's kids she had wit Alphonso ain't dead. They been adopted by this **same** couple. Celie also find out Alphonso ain't even they real daddy. Apparently, they real daddy was a black man who got lynched by a buncha white people jealous of him ballin' so hard. Then when Celie's mama had a breakdown, Alphonso swooped in and put a ring on it jus' to get summodat money 'n' property dat Celie's mama got to her name.

Back in da mothaland, Nettie try to tell Corrine dat she's da kids real aunt, but Corrine jus' like, "Psh, yeah whateva. You jus' want some of Samuel's whammy . . . bitch."

Havin' had enough of Mister's bullshit, Celie decide to join up wit' Shug and leave his ass for good. So Shug, Squeak, and Celie roll out to start a new life.

Up in Tennessee, Celie hustlin' as a tailor. She hear dat fool Albert finally gettin' his shit together; next time they see each otha, brutha even say he and Celie should get married. She like, "Fuck dat."

When Alphonso all a sudden bite da big one, Celie inherit his digs and move back to her ol' crib. Ain't all gravy, tho: now dat her woman Shug found herself a young man, Celie all kinda hurt. It take her a long-ass time to be okay wit' dat, but Celie too strong to let anythang hold her down now.

Ova in Africa, Nettie and Samuel marry afta Corrine dies. Before

they peace outta Africa, Celie's son, Adam, marry an African girl and
they all head back to da States where they drop in at Celie's house.
Nettie and Celie are reunited afta almost thirty damn years. Plus,
Shug ain't gettin' her freak on wit' dat young dude no mo', so she
and Celie back to doin' they thang. Now, da whole family togetha
again—'bout damn time somethin' good happen to deez peeps.

✌ Themes 'n' Shit ✌

COMIN' TOGETHA' (UNITY)

Da main rap of this book is showin' a woman's spiritual transformation. Da shit she go through open her mind to new perspectives on
how her life is, was, and could be in da future.

A big part of dat change is cuz of Shug Avery tellin' Celie what's
up: Errything and erryone in da world bound togetha—ain't nobody
really alone (195–196).

Knowin dat, da novel's endin' is pretty damn perfect, cuz it
showin' us dat unity in layers: Celie, who began da novel scurred,
frail, and always gettin' treated like a pile of shit, end up packin'
mad strength, independence, and new views on life. By da end, she
a "whole" person—completely unified.

For Celie, da world dun transformed too: now, it one big-ass, collective thang. Instead of writin' letters startin' wit' "Dear God" or
"Dear Nettie," she addressin' errybody and errything:

Dear God. Dear stars, dear trees, dear sky, dear peoples. Dear
Everything. Dear God. (285)

And at da end of da book, Celie experience one mo' kinda unity—a reunion wit' Nettie, Nettie's husband, and her own children, who Alphonso swiped from her when she was a kid.

GOD AND KEEPIN' IT CHURCH

Celie start out wit' a solid idea of God: what he look like, how he act, and how a brutha should worship him. To Celie, God also a thug who got her back wheneva shit get rough (3, 17).

Even tho Celie believe God is a boss-ass brutha who always gonna help a sista out, she for some reason also usin' God's name to talk 'bout painful shit. For example, she use His name when lyin' to her mama 'bout where her children be, sayin', "God took it" (2).

As Celie get mo' and mo' tight wit' Shug Avery, Shuga-mama open her eyes to thinkin' dat maybe God and religion ain't like she thought. See, Celie not only think dat you can only worship God in a church (193), but dat he also da whitest dude you ever seen (194).

Shug's version of da big G-man is a lil different: Turn out, God ain't a "he." Instead, Shug see God as an "it," and as somethin' inside of er-ryone and errything (195).

His Holiness can't even!

And usually, God gonna enter yo' life when you need it—afta beastin' through some gnarly suffering. Like Shug say when she breakin' down da God-game for Celie:

> And sometimes it just manifest itself even if you not looking, or

don't know what you looking for. Trouble do it for most folks, I think. Sorrow, lord. Feeling like shit. (195)

WHOOPIN' SOME ASS

Celie gotta tussle wit' sorrow and pain to find God, and dat ain't da only fightin' this girl gotta do. At da beginnin', Celie thinkin' she too big a pussy to fight, and don't even know how (17). Das why Mister's sis, Kate, try to get Celie amped up: a girl's gotta speak up and lay down da law (21). Only thang is, Celie too scared to do anythin', and jus' let peeps walk all over her.

At one point, Celie so pissed she can't fight for shit dat she start hatin' on people who **do** know how to fight—like Sofia. She even tell Harpo dat da only way he gonna keep Sofia in check is to do what men been doin' to Celie her whole life: abuse her. Afta Sofia find out dat Celie's been talkin' mess, she call her out on her shit, wantin' to know why Celie did what she did. Celie reply, "I say it cause I'm a fool . . . cause I'm jealous of you. I say it cause you do what I can't. . . . Fight" (40).

But at da end of da novel, Celie learn how to have mad respect for people who able to power through pain by fightin'—and realize she got da power to do da same thang.

WOMANHOOD / MANHOOD (MOTIF)

One of da biggest oppressors dat Celie and otha gals gotta beef wit' is misogyny—or da hatred of women. Da novel usin' language and events to break down dem gender stereotypes and buck dat male-focused way of thinkin'. And since we s'posed to keep dem ideas on our mind, we gonna see words 'bout womanhood and manhood all up in this bitch.

Harpo and Sofia's constant bitchin' and tusslin' often talked 'bout with terms describin' manliness: "Harpo and Sofia . . . fighting like two mens" (37).

And when Harpo hear Sofia say dat she wanna be a pallbearer for her mama, Harpo act like a lil bitch and say dat women too weak; pallbearin' is a man's job (217).

When we hearin' 'bout how bad Celie got it for Shug Avery's sexy self, we usin' a lotta manly words too. Da first time Celie see Shug, with her "long black body with it black plum nipples . . . I thought I had turned into a man" (49). Lata she say, "I notice how Shug talk and act sometimes like a man" (81).

As Celie get mo' strong and independent, she finally realize dat talkin' 'bout thangs in terms of "man" and "woman" is bullshit. Neitha of dem terms mean jack shit—cuz we all one (269).

↬ Images 'n' Symbols ↫

DA COLOR PURPLE

Da color purp is prolly da biggest symbol of this book—and it got a whole buncha different meanin': royalty, sexuality, confidence, and bein' fine as fuck. Celie think dat it's da kinda color Shug Avery would wear (20), and it's da color she uses to describe Shug's big ol' titties too (49).

Since da title of da book talkin' 'bout purple

stuff, it obviously pretty damn important. Da title basically sayin' dat dere be beauty inside of erryone and errything. And it's a beauty we best recognize if we gonna give God da credit it deserve:

> God love admiration . . . just wanting to share a good thing. I think it pisses God off if you walk by the color purple in a field somewhere and don't notice it. (196)

Purple—da color of bruises—also highlightin' da fact dat pain and sufferin' are one of da most important ways peeps come to realize dat God ain't no busta wit' a beard chillaxin in da clouds: He livin' inside each one of us. So, da color mentioned when we hearin' 'bout Sofia gettin' jacked up, covered in cuts and bruises (39, 86–87).

SEWIN' AND CLOTH

Pieces of cloth and gettin' yo' sew on sometimes actin' as a symbol up in this heezy. Otha times, it keep dat plot truckin' forward. When Nettie tryn'a tell Corrine dat she ain't never diddled Sammy's dangle, she use Corrine's memory of some fine-ass quilts to show her what's what (186–187).

Sewin' also become da main way dat Celie keep it trill and become independent in her brain, bed, and wallet (cuz she usin' it to stack change, yo) (213–214). Eventually, this sewin' shit become da way Celie express love:

> Nettie, I am making some pants for you to beat the heat in Africa. . . . You won't ever have to feel too hot and overdress again. I plan to make them by hand. Every stitch I sew will be a kiss. (214)

Me and Sofia work on the quilt. . . . Shug Avery donate her old yellow dress for scrap, and I work in a piece every chance I get. It a nice pattern call Sister's Choice. If the quilt turn out perfect, maybe I give it to her, if it not perfect, maybe I keep. (58)

✍ Shout-Outs! ✍

Givin' props to otha works dat preachin' da same truths as *The Color Purple*.

Classic

We are only as strong as we are united, as weak as we are divided.

—J. K. Rowling, *Harry Potter and the Goblet of Fire*

REMIX

Celie spend da first part of her life gettin' stepped on, pushed 'round, and straight-up disrespected. But when girl finally see how strong and badass she really be— by makin' connections wit' othas and learnin' 'bout **real love**—she starts smackin' fools 'round. Get it, girl.

✦ ✦ ✦

Classic

I believe in God, but not as one thing, not as an old man in the sky. I believe that what people call God is something in all of us. I believe that what Jesus and Mohammed and Buddha and all the rest said was right. It's just that the translations have gone wrong.

—John Lennon

REMIX

Ol J-money spittin da same jive dat Shug preachin' throughout da novel.

✦ ✦ ✦

Classic

We gon' hit 'em wit da left, hit 'em wit da right
It's a fight it's a fight head bust 'em head bust 'em.

—Three 6 Mafia, "It's a Fight"

REMIX

Pretty sho' this Sofia's theme song right hurr.

The Scarlet Letter

✦ ✠ ✦

✎ So What's the Deal? ✎

Nathaniel Hawthorne's flyest novel, an' one of da basic pillars of American lit. If you ain't in da know, *The Scarlet Letter* is da most famous book 'bout slut-shaming there is. We see a buncha peeps get all riled up 'bout somethin' dat ain't none of their damn bidness: a woman's right to get her groove on.

This book strapped wit' so many symbols—an' ways to read 'em—dat it's straight-up ridiculous, and ain't none of 'em mo' famous than Hester Prynne's big red "A" (I'm talkin' 'bout the letter, son . . .). Apparently, I ain't da only thug who like hearin' 'bout this dip shake off all da haterz dat come her way: There been multiple operas, tclc-vision shows, and movies (over ten!) givin' ol' Hester da props she deserves.

✃ Homies ✃

HESTER PRYNNE

Back in da day, Hester was married to some
dude who call himself Roger Chillingworth.
When we first meet her, tho, she already
been knocked up by anotha brutha, and now
gotta rock a big red "A" so errybody know
she committed adultery—and can hate on her
accordingly. But since Hester don't snitch, she
ain't gonna call out her baby daddy; she'd ratha jus'
beast through errybody's shit-talkin' solo. This girl's always helpin'
out otha people in da hood who been hurtin'—'specially women.

ROGER CHILLINGWORTH

Hester's husband. Even tho R-Chill ain't his real name, it's da one he
go by throughout da book. When Roger finally meet up wit' Hester
in Boston, he learn she been gettin' her freak on wit' anotha man;
and this fool **piiiiised.** So he gonna get up on dat vengeance grind
and live only to make Hester's lova suffer all day, erry day. Decked
wit' wicked street smarts, Chilly disguise himself as a doctor and hit
the scene ready to wreck dat mystery playa's life. He ain't got nothin'
on his mind but **revenge**, and end up bitter, empty, and dead at da
book's end.

PEARL

Hester's baby girl who popped out afta da scandalous affair dat got
erryone's draws in a knot. Pearl got some real attitude on her. She

always startin' so much shit in da hood dat errybody thinkin' she some sort of devil child. Shiiiiit, she actin' out so much dat da law try to take her away from Hester so they can raise her right. When Pearl all grown up at da end, word on da street is dat she got married and livin' high-class in anotha country.

ARTHUR DIMMESDALE

A righteous preacher-man who layin' down some fresh sermons on da reg. Under da surface, this fool ain't yo normal holy-rolla: he da one who been raw-doggin' Hester and be Pearl's baby daddy. But he ain't gonna tell all da hood, outta fear of bein' called out as a hypocrite: hittin' da Good Book by day, hittin' da best ass by night. Guilt weighin' down on A-money hard-core, an' he spend most of da book all tore up an' sick. Eventually, dude die in front of da whole hood afta spittin' the most legit sermon of his life.

❧ What Went Down? ☙

Out of a gnarly prison door come Hester Prynne—a woman holdin' a lil baby girl, and wearin' a big "A" stitched on her threadz. See, Hester livin' in an old-school Puritan society where erryone got real tight assholes: You keep it church, or you get yo ass taken to the streets—cuz if you fuck up, deez peeps gonna make damn sure you know it. So Hester headin' to da scaffold where errybody in da hood gathered togetha to get they hate on.

But why deez haterz hatin'? Well, it turn out Hester got knocked up by a dude who wasn't her man, and now she gotta wear dat red "A" (standin' for "adultery") so dat errytime somebody see her in da streets, they ain't lookin' at her like a person, jus' a hoochie who cain't keep her legs shut.

While she on da scaffold, Hester peep her hubby in da crowd, who goin' by da name Roger Chillingworth. Now dat he back in town, all he can think is: "Whose fuckin' kid is **dat**? An' who's been porkin' my woman?" Peeps askin' Hester who da baby daddy be, but Hester keep it hood and ain't sayin' a damn thang.

Hester get thrown back in da clink, and hubby Chillingworth come visit her, tryn'a figger out whose ass he gotta kick. Hester see jus' **how** crunk this cat gettin' and say: "Not happenin', sucka." So ol' Roger gonna hit da streets to fin' dat clown. But before he do, da doc make Hester swear she won't reveal his true identity to nobody.

Eventually, Hester get outta da slammer, and she settle in a shitty cabin on da outskirts of town, where she get by sewin' clothes for da townfolk.

Years go by, an' word on da street is dat da law gonna take Hester's daughter, Pearl, away from her, since dat little girl doin' whateva she damn well please. So Hester hit up da governor to make sure she can keep her. When Hester get to da governor's crib, he already chillin' wit' a preacher-man named Dimmesdale. She beg Dimmesdale to put in a good word to da guv and his crew, and he help a sista out. Afta dat, they decide to let Hester keep Pearl.

Pretty much errybody got mad love for Dimmesdale. Shit ain't all gravy for dat bruh, tho: Word is he been gettin' sick up in his chest. Since Chillingworth got da most wicked medical skillz in town, he set up shop in Dimmesdale's spot so he can keep an eye on him. Chilly cain't seem to figger out what wrong wit' him, tho. As time go on, Chill-dub start thinkin dat maybe what's mad-doggin' Dimmesdale ain't physical. Maybe somethin' weighin' on him real heavy, on da inside.

One night, Chillingworth creep on Dimmesdale while he catchin' him some Z's and see a big red "A" on his chest. Now Chillingworth realize what really makin' Dimmesdale pasty-ass even whiter: the guilt of puttin' it to Hester, and lettin' her take all da heat.

Dimmy decide he gonna visit da scaffold where Hester and baby Pearl got mean-mugged back in da day by da whole damn town. When Dimmesdale get there, he actually run into Hester and Pearl and let 'em know dat he feel like a real asshole for keepin' his mouth shut. Outta nowhere, a meteor light up da sky, lookin' like a big-ass "A." Chillingworth appear too, and Pearl start pointin' at him. Hester cain't believe how fucked-up Dimmesdale and Chillingworth look, and want Chillingworth to drop da vengeance game.

So Hester hit him up and ask him to stop doggin' on Dimmesdale. But Chillingworth ain't backin' down. He tell Hester he gonna do what he do, and dat she can hop off his nuts.

Hester lata meet up wit' Dimmesdale in da woods and tell him dat Chillingworth is actually her husband. Dimmesdale start wiggin' out, sayin', "You jus' telling me this NOW??" But eventually he take a chill pill. Hester convince him dat they gotta bounce, and should flow over to Europe wit' Pearl and start a new life togetha. At first, Dimmesdale jus' prancin' 'round like errything gonna be aight. But afta a lil while, he realize dat too much happened for him to jus' peace out.

Next day at Dimmesdale's sermon, shit goes south when da boat to Europe is crewin' up and Hester find out dat Chilly will be there too. She jus' cain't shake dat asshole.

Hester ain't got much time to worry, tho, cuz Dimmesdale's 'bout to get his sermonizin' on. He rocks da fuckin' mic wit' dat thang. Er-ryone agree it's da illest rhyme he eva dropped.

When he done, he do something cray—he call Hester and Pearl to da scaffold to join him. Then he tell erryone in da hood dat he got a red "A" too, rippin' off his clothes and shoutin' dat he was da one who gave it to Hester real good. Then he collapses onstage and dies. Like a bitch.

Now dat he ain't got nobody to hate on no mo', Chillingworth die. Also like a bitch. But he actually don't act like an asshole for once: He leave Pearl wit' a swole fortune. Hester peaces outta town for a little while but eventually come back, livin' out her days still wearin' dat scarlet "A." In fact, Hester keep sportin' dat letter even in da aftalife: She and Dimmesdale share a tombstone wit' a glowin' "A" on it.

∽ Themes 'n' Shit ∾

ROLLIN' SOLO VS. DEALIN' WIT' SOCIETY

Hester gettin' shat on for actin' outside da law—girl did somethin' dat da tight-ass authorities ain't feelin' and now she gotta suffer all by herself for da rest of her life: Not only do they toss her ass to da outskirts of town, but they also isolatin' her wit' they stink-eyes and shit-talkin'. Fuckin' raw deal, mayne.

Peeps always eyeballin' dat gnarly symbol on her chest. An' if you thinkin' dat time's passin' make it easier for Hester, think again. She always feel like shit errytime somebody check out dat "A": "[T]he spot never grew callous; it seemed, on the contrary, to grow more sensitive with daily torture" (89).

Haterz gonna hate, but sometimes it gonna hurt.

CHANGE

Hester, Dimmesdale, and Chilly all go through some kinda change cuz of dat scarlet letter, and it ain't for da betta. At first, Hester as fine a biddy as you ever seen. But da longer she wear da scarlet letter, da mo' jacked-up she lookin':

> As if there were a withering spell in the sad letter, her beauty, the warmth and richness of her womanhood, departed, like fading sunshine; and a gray shadow seemed to fall across her. (200)

Da scarlet letter burns like a fire, and like any flame, it gonna **spread** . . . cuz afta you blaze you gotta pass it to da left. Knowin' dat some otha fool divin' balls deep inta his woman transform Chillingworth into a straight-up monster, and it's cuz of Hester and dat "A" (164).

And da bruh dat gotta deal wit' Chillingworth's emo bulshit all day erry day? Dimmesdale. Dimmy go from high-ballin' clergyman to a broken-down bum. When Dimmesdale think he finally 'bout to get away from Chilly and dat Puritan trap, he briefly change and feel mo' alive (204).

FEELIN' TOWE UP BY GUILT AND FALSEHOOD

Dimmesdale feelin' stoopid guilty for knockin' up some biddy and not fessin' up to it. Brutha keeps it on the DL and dat shit eat away at him for years: "It is the unspeakable misery of a life so false as his . . . [that] the whole universe is false. . . . It shrinks to nothing with his grasp" (142).

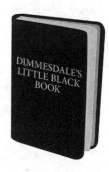

DIMMESDALE'S LITTLE BLACK BOOK

If you ain't livin' true, dat fakery gonna spread like da clap and make errything in yo life false. When Hester tryn'a convince Dimmesdale to stop bein' so hard on hisself, Dimmesdale flips out, sayin', "It is all falsehood!—all emptiness!—all death!" (183)

NOT BEIN' SURE OF DA TRUTH (AMBIGUITY)

Hawthorne pretty much beat yo' ass over da head tellin' you what his symbols mean. Prollem is, none of 'em got only **one** meanin'. And da reader ain't da only one who unsure 'bout interpretin' shit. Naw, fool. Even people **in** da novel cain't understand a damn thang anyone else sayin'.

When Dimmesdale try fess up to bangin' Hester, nobody think he talkin' on da literal. They think he jus' sayin', "We all sinners jus' like our girl Hester."

> According to these highly respectable witnesses . . . he had made the manner of his death a parable. (241)

Maybe da fact erry symbol got mo' than jus' one meanin' is symbolic in itself (see "DAT SCARLET LETTER" in Images 'n' Symbols)—Hawthorne's way of criticizin' how dem Puritan dumbasses always lookin' at thangs like they either black or white. But in reality, thangs ain't so clear-cut.

✐ Images 'n' Symbols ✐

DAT SCARLET LETTER

At da beginnin', dat red "A" reppin' adultery. Basically society stamped da word "skank" on her forehead and erryone lookin' at Hester like her sex tape jus' hit PornHub (61).

You can even say da letter turn Hester into a symbol, cuz like Chilly pointin' out, she a walkin' reminder that you should always wrap it up—to all dem Puritanical hoods, she a symbol of sin:

> The young and pure would be taught to look at her . . . as the figure, the body, the reality of sin. (83)

> Thus she will be a living sermon against sin, until the igno-minious letter be engraved upon her tombstone. (69)

Da letter also associated wit' da flames of hell:

> It assumed new terrors in their imagination, and seemed to derive its scarlet hue from the flames of the infernal pit. (74)

Readin' how da narrator talk 'bout da scarlet letter is how you jus' **know** dat none of da symbols got jus' one meaning. See, da letter start off as a tramp stamp, but afta Hester do some sweet thangs for otha people, some start thinkin' it mean "able."

> The letter was the symbol of her calling. Such helpful-ness was found in her—so much power to do and power to sympathize—that many people refused to interpret the scarlet "A" by its original signification. They said that it meant "Able"; so strong was Hester Prynne. (156)

Hell, dat "A" might even stand for "ambiguous." Hawthorne prolly gettin' all meta on our asses by **using a symbol to symbolize** dat ain't nothin' got jus' one meaning.

DA SCAFFOLD

Da scaffold and prison reppin' real nice how Puritan law got all its peeps by da balls.

> The wooden jail was already marked with weather-stains and other indications of age. . . . The rust on the ponderous iron-work of its oaken door looked more antique than anything else in the New World. Like all that pertains to crime, it seemed never to have known a youthful era. (55)

Da clink lookin' **older** than anything else in da hood, so it was prolly da first thang dem Puritans built when they landed up in M-Town. Dem tight-asses got tight-ass priorities, naw mean? But it also sayin somethin' else. Da jail ain't never been youthful ("known a youthful era"), cuz crime will always live in da heart of man; and ain't no prison cells or ball-busting lawman gonna fix dat.

THE WILD BUSH

At da beginnin' of the novel, we see a buncha uptight assholes standin' round a scary-lookin' prison. But even tho this prison —and this world—can be a real shitty place, it ain't all bad, B.

> Rooted almost at the threshold, was a wild rosebush . . . imagined to offer [its] fragrance and fragile beauty to the prisoner as he went in, and to the condemned criminal as he came forth to his doom, in token that the deep heart of Nature could pity and be kind to him. (56)

Whether you doin' some serious time or even got a death sentence, life ain't always dark. See, somethin' natural (and herbal) has grown on somethin' man-made (prison), remindin' us of somethin' important: Jus' cuz it's man's law don't mean it's nature's law. And hell—maybe its beauty can make da world's darkness a lil mo' bearable—jus' like da narrator sayin' to us readers:

> It may serve, let us hope, to symbolize some sweet moral blossom that may be found along the track, or relieve the darkening close of a tale of human frailty and sorrow. (56)

IRON

Iron symbolizin' da Puritan system of law. It's cold, hard, and so damn rigid not even da swolest thug could bend it—like da front of da prison doors at da beginning of da novel, and otha structures of da law:

> Above it rose the framework of that instrument of discipline, so fashioned as to confine the human head in its tight grasp,

and thus hold it up to the public gaze. The very ideal of igno-
miny was embodied and made manifest in this contrivance of
wood and iron. (63)

Iron also emphasizin' dat Hester surrounded by a bunch of assholes. One of da ladies talkin' mess 'bout Hester is described as "the
most iron-visaged of the old dames" (61). Scurry.

BURRRRRR

First off, Hester's hubby named **Chillingworth** and second off, he **ice-cold**.

It only get worse when he find out
his woman been getting buck-nasty wit'
someone else. Before he meet Hester,
he say: "I had lived in vain. The world
had been so cheerless! My heart was . . .
lonely and chill" (79).

BABY-GIRL PEARL

On one hand, Pearl remind Hester of her scandalous act, so it
kinda feel like lookin' afta this crazy girl is her punishment. But
on da otha hand, there somethin' merciful and lovin' 'bout Pearl
too:

Not as a name expressive of her aspect, which had nothing of
the calm, white, unimpassioned lustre that would be indicated
by the comparison. But she named the infant "Pearl," as being
of great price—purchased with all she had—her mother's only
treasure! (91)

✦ **SPARKY'S CLASSROOM** ✦

Again, the kingdom of heaven is like unto a merchant man, seeking goodly pearls:

Who, when he had found one pearl of great price, went and sold all that he had, and bought it.

—Matthew 13:45–46

Chillingworth lookin' for da truth of who knocked up his biddy like a treasure hunter searchin' for bling. And Pearl reppin' dat bling; her name is a treasure in itself.

So Roger Chillingworth—the man of skill, the kind and friendly physician—strove to go deep into his patient's bosom, delving among his principles, prying into his recollections, and probing everything with a cautious touch, like a treasure-seeker in a dark cavern. . . . He now dug into the poor clergy-man's heart like a miner searching for gold; or, rather, like a sexton delving into a grave, possibly in quest of a jewel that had been buried on the dead man's bosom, but likely to find nothing save mortality and corruption. (122, 127)

✌ Say What? ✌

Classic

To the high mountain peaks of faith and sanctity he would have climbed, had not the tendency been thwarted by the burden. . . . It kept him down, on a level with the lowest. . . . But this very burden it was that gave him sympathies so intimate with the sinful brotherhood of mankind; so that his heart vibrated in unison with theirs, and received their pain into itself, and sent its own throb of pain through a thousand other hearts, in gushes of sad, persuasive eloquence. Oftenest persuasive, but sometimes terrible! The people knew not the power that moved them thus. They deemed the young clergyman a miracle of holiness. They fancied him the mouthpiece of Heaven's messages of wisdom, and rebuke, and love. (139)

REMIX

Dimmesdale got da sickest beats cuz he actually **know** what it like to live outside of Puritan law.

✦　✦　✦

Classic

"Some men bury their secrets, thus," observed the calm physician. "True, there are such men," answered Mr. Dimmesdale. "But, not to suggest more obvious reasons, it may be that they are kept silent by the very constitution of their nature. Or—can we not suppose it—guilty as they may be, retaining, nevertheless,

a zeal for God's glory and man's welfare, they shrink from dis-
playing themselves black and filthy in the view of men; because,
thenceward, no good can be achieved by them; no evil of the past
be redeemed by better service. So, to their own unutterable tor-
ment, they go about among their fellow-creatures looking pure as
new-fallen snow; while their hearts are all speckled and spotted
with iniquity of which they cannot rid themselves." (130)

REMIX

Sometimes a playa gotta keep his past on da DL so he can keep hookin'
people up wit' da good shit. Sho as hell hurt ridin' dat beef, tho.

✦ ✦ ✦

Classic

Hester Prynne, with a mind of native courage and activity, and
for so long a period not merely estranged, but outlawed, from
society, had habituated herself to such latitude of speculation
as was altogther foreign to the clergyman. She had wandered,
without rule or guidance, in a moral wilderness; as vast, as
intricate and shadowy, as the untamed forest. . . . Her intellect
and heart had their home, as it were, in desert places, where
she roamed. . . . The scarlet letter was her passport into re-
gions where other women dared not tread. (190)

REMIX

Hester been places—on da real and da figurative—dat otha hustlas
don't have da nuts to see; and cuz of dat, she got mad street smarts
dat ain't nobody can touch.

✒ Bibliography ✒

Achebe, Chinua. *Things Fall Apart*. Edited by Francis Abiola Irele. New York: Norton, 2009.

Austen, Jane. *Pride and Prejudice*. Edited by Robert Irvine. Toronto: Broadview Literary Texts, 2002.

Bradbury, Ray. *Fahrenheit 451*. New York: Ballantine Books, 1953.

Dostoevsky, Fyodor. *Crime and Punishment*. Edited by George Gibian. New York: Norton, 1989.

Ellison, Ralph. *Invisible Man*. New York: Vintage, 1995.

Fitzgerald, F. Scott. *The Great Gatsby*. With notes and a preface by Matthew J. Bruccoli. New York: Scribner, 2003.

Golding, William. *Lord of the Flies*. New York: Perigee, 1954.

Hansberry, Lorraine. *A Raisin in the Sun*. New York: Vintage, 1994

Hawthorne, Nathaniel. *The Scarlet Letter*. New York: Signet Classic, 1959.

Lee, Harper. *To Kill a Mockingbird*. New York: Warner Books, 1960.

Melville, Herman. *Moby-Dick*. New York: Barnes & Noble Classics, 2003.

Salinger, J. D. *The Catcher in the Rye*. Boston: Little, Brown and Company, 1945.

Shakespeare, William. *Hamlet* in *The Norton Shakespeare*, 2nd ed. Edited by Stephen Greenblatt, Walter Cohen, Jean E. Howard, and Katharine Eisaman Maus. New York: Norton, 2008.

———. *Romeo and Juliet* in *The Norton Shakespeare*. 2nd ed. Edited by Stephen Greenblatt, Walter Cohen, Jean E. Howard, and Katharine Eisaman Maus. New York: Norton, 2008.

Shelley, Mary. *Frankenstein*. New York: Penguin, 2005.

Walker, Alice. *The Color Purple*. Orlando: Harvest Book Harcourt, 1982.

✦ ✚ ✦

✌ Acknowledgments ✌

Many wonderful people have been part of the Thug Notes project since day one, and without them, none of this would be possible. Thank you to our core team: Greg Edwards, Jared Bauer, Joseph Salvaggio, and Jacob Salamon. Also, a huge thanks to the amazing artists who brought these hilarious illustrations to the page: Trish Phelps, J. R. Fleming, and Kim and Tyler Rice. A massive wave of thanks to the production crew who has brought the vision of the show to life since the beginning: Richie Yau, Noah Treviño, Kate Steinhebel, Heather Horn, Kevin Chang, Jamie Parslow, Arik Cohen (you still owe us twenty dollars), and Ivan Power-Kronick. Also, huge, huge thanks to Louise and Jeffrey Davis, whose generosity knows no bounds. Thank you to the folks back home who help us when we need it most: Janell Moore, Greg and Jackie Edwards, Joe Nhiru, Nhu Kasim, and all the family back in Virginia and North Carolina. Also thanks to Shelley Barash Bauer, Fia Bauer, Debbie Goldberg, and Mikey Vidal. Thank you to the awesome team over at Moss, Levy and Hartzheim for helping us when we needed it: Craig, Eddie, and Marina. Thank you to our shysty agent, Ethan Bassoff, and our wonderful champion at Vintage, Tim O'Connell this book is because of you! Thank you to Angela Lin, who helped keep the show going when times were tough. Thanks to our many amazing teachers who helped us fall in love with literature. And finally, we want to thank our amazing fans all around the world who show their love and support every day—our well-read ballas. You mean everything to us.

✦ ✚ ✦

✎ Illustration Credits ✑

All composite images were created by Jacob S. Salamon with images found in the public domain or otherwise licensed from Shutterstock, as listed below.

To Kill a Mockingbird: page 24 (Scout face) Everett Collection; page 27 (Scout face) Everett Collection, (Scout outfit) Everett Collection, (Jem) frescomovie, (dill) Serdar Tibet, (house) Scott Prokop, (kids running) Sergey Novikov; page 28 (Atticus face) Dennis Cox, (woman with "HATE" sign) Stokkete; page 29 (chair) dennnis, (rug) zzveillust, (joint) Stepan Kapl, (Boo face) Elzbieta Sekowska; page 31 (Scout face) Everett Collection, (eyeglasses) Pashin Georgiy, (Tom Rob face) Ryan Jorgensen-Jorgo, (Boo face) Elzbieta Sekowska; page 33 (arm in sling) fotofreaks, (Boo face) Elzbieta Sekowska, (hat) Tshirt Designs, (car) Malivan_Iuliia; page 35 (bird) hopko, (boombox) stuart_ford, (rings) Arnon Fueangphiban, (chains) Alexander V Evstafyev, (sparkles) In-Finity

The Great Gatsby: page 61 (chaise) Jose Ignacio Soto, (George outfit) Ysbrand Cosijn, (Myrtle portrait) Olena Zaskochenko, (Myrtle dress and Tom outfit) Anastasia Mazeina, (champagne flutes) gresei, (chandelier) StudioSmart; page 62 (Jay Gatsby outfit) Ysbrand Cosijn; page 63 (joints) Stepan Kapl, (Nick outfit) Everett Collection, (shades) Stefanina Hill, (rolls) Dashenzia; page 67 (Myrtle portrait) Olena Zaskochenko, (Myrtle dress and bouquet) Segoya

Frankenstein: or, The Modern Prometheus: page 76 (monster) luxorphoto; page 78 (snow hat) benchart, (rope) creatOR76, (spinners) Tetiana Yurchenko, (sled) Mascha Tace, (sparkle) Wiktoria Pawlak, (monster) luxorphoto; page 81 (monster) luxorphoto; page 84 (heaven) Ivan Ponomarev, (middle finger) Goldenarts, (monster) luxorphoto; page 85 (monster) luxorphoto; page 89 (tombstone) VectorShots, (tear drop) OrelPhoto

Invisible Man: page 94 (narrator face) John Penezic, (megaphone) VikaSuh, (shoes) Baimieng; page 97 (narrator face) John Penezic, (belt) Vivi o, (outfit) Jack Frog, (bucket) Netkoff; page 98 (hair) Arak Rattanawijittakorn, (outfit top) Nejron Photo; page 99 (Ras face) Ryan Jorgensen-Jorgo, (outfit) Juliya Shangarey, (highway silhouette) Cata-Vic, (1930s Manhattan skyline) Natalia Bratslavsky, (tourists) Boguslaw Mazur, (tourist accessories) WINS86, (spear) 3drenderings; page 100 (book) badahos, (painters) Andrey_Popov and auremar, (pattern) Apolinarias, ("history" label) Teamarwen; page 101 (narrator face) John Penezic, (shoes) Baimieng, ("Hello" sticker) Gunnar Pippel, (plate) AlenKadr, (pork chops) Jacek Chabraszewski, (grits) Vizual Studio, (art deco elements on placard) H Cooper

Lord of the Flies: page 110 (Piggy) Vasiliy Koval, (sun) mmar, (glasses) Photology1971, (cheeseburger) Orfeev; page 112 (gavel) Iraidka, (conch) andrey oleynik; page 114 (pig head) SoRad, (grass) ekler; page 116 (pig head) SoRad, (pig body) Vmaster, (noose) Hurst Photo; page 117 (dam) Subidubi, (face/mask) aastock, (monster) IvanNikulin; page 119 (glasses) Photology1971; page 120 (grass) ekler, (cigar) Alhovik

Moby-Dick: page 134 (Ahab clothes) Petrafler, (tiki drink) Guseletova, (sunglasses) TheRenderFish, (couple in bed) Marcos Mesa Sam Wordley, (tattoos) sunlight77; page 136 (calendar) Viktor Jarema, (TV scene) Tomacco; page 137 (fire ring) Olga Nikonova, (pentagram and horns) Marek Hlavac; page 139 (tuna can) BimXD

A Raisin in the Sun: pages 148, 154, 156 (Walter) PathDoc

Hamlet: page 166 (ticket art) Macrovector; page 169 (foil sword) Aleks Melnik; page 171 (ghost body) SDL, (recliner) John Langton; page 172 (headphones) Christos Georghiou

Fahrenheit 451: page 182 (fire hat) VectorShots, (Guy Montag) mimagephotography; page 183 (model citizen head) upthebanner, (ashtray) Levent Konuk, (lounge chair) 1507kot; page 185 (fire hat) VectorShots, (Guy Montag) mimagephotography; page 190 (boy on left) karelnoppe, (boy on right) Veronica Louro

The Catcher in the Rye: page 200 (Holden face) Ilike, (scarf) Webspark; page 206 (chalkboard details) wang song; page 209 (Holden face) Ilike, (scarf) Webspark; page 210 (signs) WimStock; page 212 (Holden face) Ilike, (chains) ALEXANDER V EVSTAFYEV, (silhouette) alextrims

Crime and Punishment: page 218 (middle finger vector) Pirx Yazon, (money counter) Webspark; page 224 (Earth) grmarc; page 225 (Jay Z) s_bukley

Things Fall Apart: page 235 (Okonkwo face) Warren Goldswain, (Jenga pieces) maimu, (Okonkwo outfit pattern) Olesya Kuznetsova; page 241 (Okonkwo face) Warren Goldswain, (Okonkwo outfit pattern) Olesya Kuznetsova, (yelling mouth) Danomyte, (African man) Tish1; page 244 (Okonkwo face) Warren Goldswain, (mouth) dedMazay, (bodybuilder) Digital-Clipart; page 245 (salsa packet) Photo Melon

The Color Purple: page 252 (Shug) tobkatrina; page 254 ("Return to Sender" stamp) ducu59us; page 255 (Sofia) Chris from Paris, (Harpo) PathDoc, (arm) vishstudio, (ball gag) Margarita Sh; page 259 (man's body) RetroClipArt; page 260 (combat body) Anton Brand

SPARKY SWEETS, PHD

Dr. Sparky Sweets was recognized by the National Association of Scholars in 2013 for his unique approach to education. Although well-versed in all areas of the lit-game, he finds his biggest inspiration in the works of Fyodor Dostoevsky and other narratives full of existential angst. The good doctor is portrayed by comedian Greg Edwards, who hosts the weekly comedy show "The Workout Room" in L.A.'s Koreatown.

www.gregcomedy.com

WISECRACK

Wisecrack is a Los Angeles–based media collective run by academics and comedians who want to help people know their shit. Their other shows include 8-Bit Philosophy, Earthling Cinema, and Boss Bitches of History.

www.wisecrack.co

✦ ✚ ✦